The

Umbria

Complete guide to the monuments,
art and traditions of the region

BONECHI

© Copyright by Casa Editrice Bonechi
Via Cairoli, 18/b - 50131 Firenze - Italia
Tel. +39 055576841 - Fax +39 0555000766
E-mail: bonechi@bonechi.it
Internet: www.bonechi.it
          www.bonechi.com

Printed in Italy by Centro Stampa Editoriale Bonechi.

Text by cura di Giuliano Valdes - Editing Studio, Pisa.

English translation: Rhiannon Lewis Pucci

The publishers and the author wish to thank Professor Bruno Dozzini and
Dr. Guido Lemmi of Perugia for their kind assistance in the preparation
of this book

PHOTO CREDITS :

Andrea Angelucci: pages 25; 49 above; 50.

Azienda di Promozione Turistica del Ternano: page 125.

Gaetano Barone: pages 4; 6; 8 above; 13; 14 above; 17; 20; 21; 23; 26; 35;42; 45; 48;
49 below; 51; 53; 55; 56; 61; 63 below; 64; 65; 69; 71 above;72; 75; 77; 79; 81; 82;
84 on the left; 91 below; 92; 94; 96; 97; 98; 99; 100 below;101; 102; 103; 104; 105;
106 above; 110; 113; 122; 126; 127; 129; 130; 131; 132 below; 135; 138 above; 140.

Stefano Cellai: pages 8 below; 9; 10; 30; 36 above; 38 above, 39; 43; 84 on the right;
87; 88; 100 above; 106 below; 138 below.

Adriano Cioci: page 41 below.

Foto Scala: pages 16; 73.

Paolo Giambone: pages 115; 137.

Giuliano Valdes - Editing Studio, Pisa: pages 63 above; 139.

Andrea Pistolesi: pages 14 below; 15; 19; 27; 28; 29; 31; 37; 38 below; 41 above;
57; 58; 59; 60; 67; 83; 91 above; 93; 109; 111; 114; 117; 118; 119; 120; 121;
123; 132 above; 133.

Padre Gerhard Ruf: pages 32; 33; 34; 36 below.

Studio Fotografico Gavirati, Gubbio: page 71 below.

ISBN 978-88-8029-165-7

* * *

INTRODUCTION

HISTORY

Archaeological remains dating back to the Palaeolithic *and* Neolithic *periods document Man's presence in Umbria since the most remote times. On the other hand, the history of this region must obviously date back thousands of years, given its geographical position - at the centre of the Italian peninsular - forming a dividing line between Northern and Southern Italy, as well as being a watershed between the Tyrrhenian and Adriatic Seas. The first Oscan-Umbrian colonies were formed in the 11C BC., during the same period that the town settlements appeared, initially extending far beyond the region's present boundaries. Later, as other tribes moved into the region - above all, the Etruscans, - but also the Celts, Piceni and the Sabines, the Umbrians were forced to reside in more compact and restricted territory. The seven bronze* Eugubine Tablets *(3C-1C BC.) give indisputable proof of the existence of the ancient language of the Umbrian people, as well as furnishing an interesting insight into the life of those times. The presence of the Etruscans in Umbria, is thoroughly documented at Perugia and Orvieto (*Volsinii*). The Roman colonization of Umbria, which took place after they had beaten the Etruscan, Samnite and Gaulish confederates at Sentino (*295 BC.*), led to the decline of the Umbrian civilization which gradually became more integrated with that of Rome. This came about as a result of the founding of new towns and important public works and buildings, but above all by the conferring of Roman* Civitas *upon the Umbrian people (*90 BC.*). The magnitude of the work the Romans accomplished in Umbria cannot fail to be noticed by even the least observant of visitors. The ruins of many roads, bridges, temples and entire cities (*Carsulae*) and also theatres, amphitheatres, walls and town gates, demonstrates the Romans' skill as builders and engineers (a well known example being the splendid irrigation system in which the waters of the Velino river were diverted into those of the Nera, creating the Cascata delle Marmore). The* Early Christian period *marked not only the beginning of a new faith but also foreshadowed the construction of splendid churches and basilicas, which make Umbria one of the most important regions in terms of monuments and landmarks. These also provided the basis for the innovative, and in a certain sense, revolutionary religious uprisings, defended by the Western Monasticism of St Benedict and the Franciscan movement, which came into being with the advent of the great saint of Assisi. Meanwhile, the various struggles between the Goths and the Byzantines, and the later arrival of the Lombards, finally led to the territories of Umbria being divided up between the Lombards (the Dukedom of Spoleto) and the Byzantines, who took control of Perugia, Narni and Terni.*
Between the 8C and the 9C, as a result of land donated by the Franks, the Church was able to gain control of the territories which had been under Lombard and Umbro-Byzantine control. From the 11C onwards, the setting up of free communes marked a greater awareness of their individuality on the part of the major towns (Perugia, Assisi, Spoleto, Foligno, Terni, Gubbio, Città di Castello). At the same time, this period foreshadowed the beginning of bitter feuds between the Guelphs and the Ghibellines, paladines of the Papacy and the Empire. During the 14C *and the* 15C, *in spite of the strong domination of noble lords (Baglioni at Perugia, Atti at Todi, Trinci at Foligno, Monaldeschi at Orvieto) and the presence of "condottieri" (leaders of mercenary troops) (Braccio Fortebraccio of Montone, Niccolò and Iacopo Piccinino, the Gattamelata), the region became gradually more integrated with the territories controlled by the Papacy. Between the* 15C *and the* 18C, *in spite of some attempts at rebellion against the Papal government (the so-called "Salt War" of 1540 at Perugia being a famous example), Umbria seems to have taken an aloof stance towards the upheavals of that time, even though some remarkable and innovative trends (above all in art and architecture) were taking place in the region. At the time of Napoleon Bonaparte's arrival in Italy, Umbria, between 1798 and 1799, was part of the Roman Republic. Afterwards, it became a part of the Papal State once again, as the result of the re-establishment of the Viennese Assizes (1815). After frequent rebellious uprisings, which fuelled the Risorgimento movement in the region, Umbria was annexed to the new Italian Kingdom in 1860.*

ART HISTORY

Burial grounds, necropolises, tombs and the ruins of polygonal walls are just some of the numerous and highly significant features, which remain as a result of the Etruscan period in Umbria. Of great historical importance are the **Etruscan Arch,** *the* **Porta Marzia** *and the* **Ipogeo** *(underground tomb)* **dei Volumni** *at* **Perugia.** *At* **Orvieto** *can be found the* **Necropolises of the Cannicella** *and the* **Crucifix of Tufa.**

The Romanization of Umbria resulted in both major public buildings and important centres being erected. Such is the case of the **Via Flaminia** *(parts of which are paved with large blocks of stone) and the ancient ruins of* **Carsulae.** *There are numerous* **Theatres,** *the most outstanding being those of* **Gubbio** *and* **Spoleto;** *Amphitheatres (Spoleto, Assisi, Spello, Todi), Bridges (Narni, Spoleto), Temples and* **Mausoleums (Assisi, Gubbio, Campello sul Clitunno).**

As a result of the first Christian uprisings and the establishing of primitive communities of believers, sacred buildings and Early Christian basilicas were erected. These include the **Basilica of the Saviour** *at* **Spoleto** *(4C); the Temple of Clitunno, re-converted into the Church of the Saviour (4C); the* **Church of S. Angelo** *(6C) and the* **Basilica of St Peter** *(10C) at* **Perugia.**

The remarkable flourishing of the Romanesque style in Umbria is often found accompanied by motifs and features of Lombard design. Worthy of note are the marvellous **Cathedral of Spoleto** *(12C) and the* **Church of S. Eufemia** *(12C); the* **Cathedral of Assisi** *(12-13C), the* **Churches of St Michael** *and* **St Sylvester** *at* **Bevagna** *(late 12C) and the* **Church of the Saviour** *at* **Terni** *(parts of which are Early Christian).*

At Assisi, the **Basilica of St Francis,** *a shining masterpiece of the Umbrian transition style (13C), represents a milestone in the art of this region, due to its wonderful frescoes painted by Giotto, Cimabue, Pietro Lorenzetti and Simone Martini. The Basilica inspired the building of numerous churches at that time, both within the town (e.g.* **St Clare's)** *and elsewhere (***St Francis in Terni, St Francis "al Prato" in Perugia***).*

The **Cathedral of Orvieto,** *a famous example of the architectural style of Maitani, represents one of the most vivid examples of the Gothic style in Umbria (13C-14C). Other examples of Gothic architecture are the* **People's Palace** *and the* **Captain's Palace** *(both 13C) at* **Todi;** *the* **Priors' Palace** *(13C) at* **Perugia** *and the* **Consuls' Palace** *at* **Gubbio** *(14C). The* **bas-reliefs of the façade** *of the Cathedral of* **Orvieto** *(by Maitani) and the* **sculptures of the Fontana Maggiore** *at* **Perugia** *(Nicola and Giovanni*

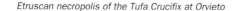

Etruscan necropolis of the Tufa Crucifix at Orvieto

Pisano) are considered to be the most famous examples of Gothic figurative art in Umbria.

Considerable evidence of the Renaissance period can be seen in the Bramante-influenced **Temple of St Mary of Solace** (16C) at Todi; the **Ducal Palace** at **Gubbio** (15C) - the architect Laurana used the Ducal Palace of Urbino as a model; the **Porta San Pietro** and the **Oratory of San Bernardino** (**Perugia,** both dating from the 15C); the **Spada Palace** at **Terni**, the last work of Antonio da Sangallo the Younger (16C).

Renaissance painting in Umbria boasts contributions made by the great Tuscan masters such as Benozzo Gozzoli, Filippo Lippi, Beato Angelico (**Foligno** and **Orvieto**) and Masolino da Panicale (**Todi, Church of San Fortunato**). The beautiful frescoes which adorn the **Cappella Nuova** of the Cathedral of **Orvieto** are the works of another Tuscan artist, Luca Signorelli. The most important painters of the Umbrian school are Pietro Vannucci (Perugino), whose works are exhibited in the **National Gallery of Umbria** and in the **Collegio del Cambio** at **Perugia** and Bernardino di Betto (Pinturicchio) whose wonderful frescoes can be seen at the **Cappella Baglioni** (**Church of S. Maria Maggiore** at **Spello**).

GEOGRAPHICAL BACKGROUND

Surrounded by Tuscany, Lazio and the Marches, Umbria is one of the smallest regions of Italy (8456 sq.kms) and is the only one whose boundaries do not touch the sea. Nonetheless, there is a wide range of different landscapes to be found here, ranging from the Apennine mountains and the sweeping expanses of hilly ranges, to the large valleys and broad lowlands. All these multifarious landscapes combine to form an overall picture of such scenic beauty that the definition of Umbria as "the Green heart of Italy" would seem to be an extremely suitable one. The inland basins are all tributaries of the **Tiber,** which runs in a north-south-easterly direction, making up the watershed between the Tyrrhenian and Adriatic Seas.

The **Umbrian-Marches-Apennine** runs from the **Bocca Trabaria** to the **Forca Canapine** and comprises **Mt Catria, Mt Pennino** and **Mt Vettore**, which forms part of the **Sibillini mountain** range. In fact, the Apennines themselves run along the same course, changing direction on the reliefs of **Mt Urbino, Mt Subasio** and **Mt Coscerno**. At the mouth of the upper **Valtiberina**, between the river courses of the **Tiber**, the **Topino** and the **Nera**, lie the lower reaches of the **Martani Mountains.** The inland lowlands were formed as a result of the silting up of ancient lakes during the Quaternary period (a well-known example being the immense Lake Tiberino which once stretched from Sansepolcro to Terni): worthy of note are the plains of Gubbio, Gualdo Tadino, Norcia and Terni.

As well as the Valtiberina (in the north), two other valleys worthy of note are the **Valle Umbra**, between Torgiano and Spoleto, along which runs the **Marroggia**, the **Clitunno**, the **Topino** and the **Chiascio** rivers, and the wild **Valnerina** valley, nestling between picturesque gorges up until the point where the Terni plain opens out.

As well as the other sources of water which cover the surface area (widespread examples of the Karst phenomena are to be found on the slopes of the Sibillini mountains), mention should be made of the river **Paglia**, the river **Nestore** and the lakes. These lakes include the enormous **Lake Trasimeno** (the largest of the region), **Lake Piediluco** and the artificial basins of **Corbara, Alviano** and **Valfabbrica**.

The population of Umbria is just over 800,000 inhabitants which is evenly distributed throughout the region. There are only two provincial capitals: **Perugia** and **Terni**. However, there are also many large towns and places of great artistic, urban and historical interest. These include **Foligno, Spoleto, Città di Castello, Gubbio, Assisi, Orvieto, Todi** and **Norcia**.

The climate of Umbria is influenced by its geographical position, being so close to the Apennine mountains and relatively far away from the sea (in fact, none of its boundaries touches the sea at all). Therefore, in winter it is cold and damp, while in summer, the weather is hot and often sultry. The annual rainfall is around 800mm. The lower reaches of the valleys are sometimes steeped in mist and fog. Although there are only occasional and sporadic spells of snow along the plains and across the hills, it falls more frequently and lingers longer along the higher reaches of the Apennine mountains.

A view of the the Springs of Clitunnus, near Trevi, well-known since ancient times

PROTECTED AREAS

As a result of renewed interest and growing sensibility throughout Italy towards the protection and conservation of the countryside and the environmental heritage, Umbria is having to conform with the proposals put forward by the other Italian regions. With the need to keep in line with international guide-lines towards safeguarding natural beauty spots and wildlife, the relevant regional organizations, after having deliberated the ratification of necessary urban measures, are now working towards the setting up of nature parks and reserves.

*The protected areas in Umbria are classified into three groups: Nature Parks of regional interest coming under the Urban and Territorial Plan of the Region of Umbria (**Group A**); Water Parks listed in the Urban and Territorial Plan of the Region of Umbria (**Group B**); Areas of particular naturalistic and environmental interest listed in the Urban and Territorial Plan of the Region of Umbria (**Group C**). The following areas are included in Group A: the **Sibillini mountains, Marcite di Norcia, Mt Cucco, Gola del Corno del Catria, Mt Subasio**, the **Coscerno - Aspra - L'Aspro mountain range**, the **ilex groves of the Colle la Bernara and Mt Solenne**. The following areas are included in Group B: the **river course of the Tiber, Lake Corbara, Lake Alviano**, the **River Nera, Valnerina, Lake Piediluco**. The following areas are classified under Group C: **Mountain of Pietralunga, Mt Tezio - Mt Acuto, Mt Ingino - Mt Foce, Mountain of Gualdo Tadino, Mt Malbe**, the **Plains of Colfiorito and Ricciano, Marshes of Colfiorito**, the **Plains of Ricciano**, the **mountains between Foligno and Spoleto**, the **Fountains of Clitunno**, the **ilex groves of Sassovivo**, the **hills and islands of Trasimeno, Lake Trasimeno, Mt Pausillo, Mt Peglia, Martani mountains - Mt Torre Maggiore**, the **pine forests of the Valle del Serra**, the **mountains of Allerona, Mt Croce di Serra** and the **ilex groves of Amelia**.*

THE SPA TOWNS

*Even though Umbria does not touch the sea, there is a plentiful and well distributed supply of water throughout the region. Six types of mineral waters are to be found here, a factor which brings importance and wealth to the six spa towns from which they originate. The most famous spas of the region are those of San Gemini, the spa buildings being situated in the small village of San Gemini Fonte, near the impressive ruins of the Roman settlement of **Carsulae**. **Sangemini** water is slightly effervescent and contains traces of calcium, chlorine and sodium. It is recommended in the treatment of children's diseases and for disorders of the digestive system. It*

is also used to cure metabolic disorders and urinary infections. **Fabia** *mineral water, an alkaline water containing bicarbonate, is recommended for the treatment of both liver and metabolic disorders.*
In the district surrounding Terni, at Acquasparta, *one comes across the springs of* **Amerino** *and* **Furapane**. *The former have a medium mineral content and contain calcium carbonate (or calcite). They are recommended in the treatment of gout and kidney stones and also for disorders of the joints, muscles and the metabolic system. The latter are recommended for the treatment of liver and digestive disorders.*
Near Città di Castello *can be found the springs of* **Fontecchio** *mineral water. This has a medium mineral content and contains alkaline bicarbonate sulphide. It is recommended for orthopaedic and pulmonary disorders. It has also proved successful in the treatment of arthritis, digestive and gynaecological disorders and also for vascular infections. The spa buildings of* **San Faustino** *are to be found at* Massa Martana. *The mineral water here is alkaline and contains bicarbonate. It is used for treating metabolic disorders, liver and kidney stones and infections of the digestive and intestinal systems. Even* Assisi *has a small spa centre of ancient Roman origins at* **Santo Raggio**. *The water is low in mineral content and contains alkaline bicarbonate. It is used for treating gout, uricaemia, lithiasis of the urinary system, dyspepsia and infections of the gastro-intestinal systems. At* Nocera Umbra *one can find the spas of* **Angelica, Flaminia** *and* **Cacciatore**. *The waters of Cacciatore are low in mineral content and are recommended for infections of the digestive system, gastro-enteritis and urinary disorders.*

ECONOMY

Once a predominantly rural region, Umbria has managed to conserve (despite the industrial revolution of the twentieth century) the right balance between town and country. Nowadays, its economy is drawn from activities in the service sector, followed by those of industry and agriculture. The plethora of natural water sources has, in fact, led to rapid and widespread industrialization in the southern parts of the region (Terni and Narni), where iron and steel works, metal and mechanical industries and chemical plants have been set up (even though they have suffered a certain decline in the last ten years). The industrial district around Perugia has witnessed a growth in both the food and textile industries and, in a more generic sense, that of the building industry. The Upper Valtiberina, the districts around Gubbio, Gualdo and Foligno are also relatively thriving industrial areas. The depopulation of the countryside has affected the agricultural industry of Umbria to a lesser degree than many other regions. Here, highly prized and specialized crops (e.g. wine and olives) are grown, as well as a considerable amount of cereals and vegetables. Many farms have recently joined the "Agriturismo" scheme, a decidedly successful feature of the wide-ranging accommodation facilities on offer in Umbria.
The handicraft industry is a tradition which goes back over hundreds of years. The manufacturing of ceramics is carried out in Deruta, Orvieto, Todi, Gubbio, Città di Castello, Assisi, Gualdo Tadino and Umbertide. Majolica pottery, clay vases ("buccheri" - black delicately thin Etruscan ceramics, usually incised or painted), earthenware pitchers, jars and vases are produced in Gualdo Tadino, Orvieto, Castel Viscardo, Ficulle and Città di Castello. Wrought iron handicrafts is a particularly thriving industry at Gubbio, Assisi, Orvieto, Città della Pieve, Magione, Passignano, Sellano and Norcia. Copperware is to be found at Magione. Precious stones and gold jewellery are produced in Orvieto and at Perugia, Assisi, Gubbio, Terni and Todi. An important part of the handicraft industry is that dealing with furniture restoration and carpentry; the most important workshops being those located at Perugia, Assisi, Gubbio, Todi, Città di Castello, Orvieto, Foligno, Corciano, Montecchio, Massa Martana and Norcia. At Gubbio, Assisi and Foligno, musical instruments are both produced and restored. The highly specialized craft of Irish lace making can be seen on Isola Maggiore (upon Lake Trasimeno). Lace is also manufactured at the riverside towns of Castiglione del Lago and Tuoro sul Trasimeno, as well as in Panicale. Orvieto, on the other hand, as well as being famous for its lace production, is also famous for crochet work. Embroidery, table centrepieces and curtains are to be found throughout the region; the main producing centres being Perugia, Panicale, Città di Castello, Assisi and Orvieto. Textile handicrafts can be found at Cascia, Città di Castello, Marsciano,

7

Local ceramic crafts at Gubbio

Wood carving at Orvieto

Montefalco, Spoleto and Spello. At San Feliciano di Magione, rush matting made from the reeds of the nearby shores of Lake Trasimeno is produced. San Nicolò di Celle is noted for the production of chairs. Glass is produced at Perugia and Assisi (stained glass windows) and at Piegaro (demijohns and flasks). Marble sculptures and sandstone articles are produced throughout the region, whilst costumes and masks are typical of such towns as Perugia, Terni and Marsciano. Basket work, bags and hand-painted lampshades are found in Assisi, while Orvieto is famous for its production of umbrellas. Figurines and sculptures are made at Gubbio, Foligno and Spoleto. In Spoleto, riding enthusiasts can also find saddles and harnesses. At Città di Castello, certain publications are still published using the monotype printing system.

A painstaking re-appraisal of the whole tourist sector in general, leading to more efficient standards in accommodation facilities, together with improved road networks better suited to cope with the high flow of traffic, are factors which have made the tourist industry one of the most important contributors to the Umbrian economy. In Umbria there is an awareness that even though the major towns and acclaimed centres of historical and artistic interest (Perugia, Orvieto, Assisi, Gubbio, Spoleto, Todi, Città della Pieve) provide the main tourist attractions, the "minor" centres also play an essential role in boosting the region's tourist industry. This is the case with such towns as Città di Castello, Passignano sul Trasimeno, Castiglione del Lago, Bettona, Deruta, Bevagna, Montefalco, Spello, Terni, San Gemini, Amelia, Narni, Ferentillo and, to the same degree, Gualdo Tadino, Nocera Umbra, Foligno, Cascia and Norcia. Even though these places might seem to be of secondary importance when compared to the more traditional tourist destinations, they are of fundamental importance if one wants to make a thorough and exhaustive visit to one of the most beautiful regions of Italy.

TRADITIONAL FESTIVALS AND EVENTS

A land of traditional fairs and religious and cultural festivals, Umbria is above all the cradle of religious zeal and fervour, whose origins are lost in the mists of time. It is well known that the roots of Western Monasticism can be traced back to the figure of St Benedict of Norcia, who lived between the 5C and 6C. An equally important figure was his sister St Scholastica, who was also canonized as a saint. St Francis and St Clare of Assisi, S. Ubaldo of Gubbio and the humble figure of Rita Lotti Mancini "the Rose of Roccaporena" are yet further examples of why this region has been nicknamed the land of saints.

The intermingling of both the sacred and the profane constitutes a unique element, which lies at the heart of all the main traditional festivals of Umbria. However, these are not only put on as a folk attraction for the enjoyment of sightseers and outsiders. They are in fact part of a cultural and religious heritage, which is deeply rooted in the consciousness of the Umbrian people. Throughout the region, numerous events based on the theme of the Passion of Christ *are held to celebrate the end of Lent. There are also numerous* **Processions of the Dead Christ**, *whose themes are based on the ancient hymns of praise (or lauds) written by Francis of Assisi and another of Umbria's important figures, the mystical poet Iacopone of Todi. In this region, history, religion and tradition all come together to provide the basis for some highly spectacular events. An example of this is the* **Corsa dei Ceri** *(candle race) held at Gubbio on the 15th of May, the eve of the patron saint's day* (S. Ubaldo). *On this occasion the town cheers on the "ceraioli" (candle bearers) which represent each of the ancient town corporations. Each team carries an enormous polygonal wooden tower, topped with a wax saint (Ubaldo, George and* Anthony the Abbot) *on its shoulders. The lively race finishes at the Basilica of S. Ubaldo on Mt Ingino. This tradition, which is perhaps incorrectly defined as a "race" (as it is not a real competition because S. Ubaldo must always be the first to arrive at the Basilica) is linked, according to some hypotheses, to an episode from medieval history. It is supposed to commemorate the day on which the Eugubines, with the help of S. Ubaldo, fought back a confederation of rival*

The Giostra della Quintana at Foligno

9

The characteristic "flower carpets" of Corpus Domini at Spello

communes who had surrounded the town. The event is also rooted in pagan ritual, harking back to expiatory rites and favourable auspices at the advent of spring. On the last Sunday of May, Gubbio also hosts the **Palio della Balestra**, where medieval contests and customs are once again brought to life. Even the traditional event of **Cantarmaggio,** whose origins date back to ancient times, contains ancient pagan themes. Mention should also be made of the **Calendimaggio** (spring festival), which takes place in Assisi between the end of April and the beginning of May. A parade in historical costumes and a unique contest between the two opposing town "districts" animate the birthplace of St Francis with colours, sounds and lights, as it prepares to welcome another spring. During the last ten days of May, Cascia is also lit up with torch light processions and religious fervour for the celebrations dedicated to **St Rita**. These conclude with a historical procession from Roccaporena to the modern Basilica. To celebrate **Whitsuntide** and **Corpus Domini**, pavements, cobbled streets and piazzas are filled with the magnificent colours of spring and the impending summer. These colours are provided by the flower carpets ("infiorate") which are laid down along the streets transforming medieval town centres into a phantasmagorical mosaic of multi-coloured petals. Amongst the most famous "infiorate" is that of Spello. In late spring, there are numerous events taking place in Umbria. Amongst the festivals associated with folklore and local traditions are the **Corsa dell'Anello** (ring tournament) and the nocturnal **Historical Pageant** at Narni; the **Cantamaggio** at Terni; the **Festa della Palombella** (horse race); the **Processione del Corporale** and the **Historical Pageant** at Orvieto. Even in autumn, many important events are held such as the **Giostra della Quintana** at Foligno on the second Sunday in September. Here, various town districts take part in jousting tournaments, dressed in 17C costumes. A **Jousting Tournament** is also held at Narni, while at the beginning of November in Perugia, the famous **Fiera dei Morti (All Souls' Fair)** is held, where delicious confectionery and sweets are to be found on sale.

LOCAL CUISINE

Simple, wholesome and home-made dishes constitute a salient feature common to all the specialities of Umbrian gastronomy. The cuisine of this region takes full advantage of all the "raw materials" and ingredients provided by the "Green heart of Italy", and it is these ingredients which make the local dishes both appetizing and delicious. As Umbria is fundamentally a rural area, an abundance of natural produce has always been readily available here. Amongst the pulses, which together with a vast range of fruit and vegetables are to be found in great abundance in this rich and fertile land, note should be made of the highly-acclaimed lentils of Castelluccio. Amongst the various cereals, mention should be made of the outstanding farro *(farley)* which, together with the onion *is widely used in the preparation of soups. Another outstanding product found in Umbria is the* truffle, *a rare, highly prized, tasty ingredient of regional dishes, which acts as a delicious accompaniment to hors d'oeuvres, first courses, main dishes and even desserts.* White *truffles (from Upper Valtiberina and Gubbio) and* black *truffles (from the Valnerina) give a highly distinctive flavour to Umbrian cuisine and should not be missed, even though they are very expensive. How can one, in this brief introduction to local produce, forget to mention the* olive oil *of Umbria? The areas in which this highly prized and specialized method of cultivation is most widespread are the districts around Spoleto, the anti-Apennines of the Assisi region, the hills of Trasimeno, the hills around the Teri basin and the lower reaches of the Nera Valley.* Chestnuts, *and above all the large and delicately flavoured marron chestnuts, were once a part of the staple diet of the population. Today, they are widely used in the preparation of confectionery (even on an industrial scale) and all the typical sweets and desserts of the region. If the Valnerina is deservedly famous for the beauty of its natural environment and landscapes, one should not overlook the ancient art of the "norcini" (pork butchers of Norcia). In the upper valley, at the birthplace of St Benedict and St Scholastica, the Norcians prepare pork specialities according to ancient methods.* Excellent hams, salami *and various types of* sausages like "mazzafegato" *(a sausage spiced with a mixture of pine nuts, pork liver, candied orange, sugar and raisins), and* mules' testicles *take pride of place in a gastronomic tradition which has always been carried out on an artisan level. However, today these specialities have come to be an acknowledged feature of the whole valley. Sources of natural water (or "sister water" as St Francis called it) are widely dispersed throughout the region, as the presence of lakes and rivers amply demonstrates. This fact accounts for the wide variety of* fish dishes *to be found in Umbrian cuisine* (perch or bass, carp, trout, eels, tench, roach, grey mullet and pike). *Pride of place amongst the hors d'oeuvres is taken by an excellent range of* cold cuts - hams, sausages and "capocollo" (neck of beef) *accompanied by delicious* canapés *(with* truffles *or* chicken livers), fritters *or* flat bread baked with olive oil *(flavoured with* sage *or with* onions) *and* pizzas *(amongst which excels the well-known* "torta al testo perugina" *-unleavened bread baked on a stone slab- with ham or sausages). In a region noted for its pasta production (both on an industrial scale and also the home-made variety), the first course dishes are obviously outstanding. Here we find* "strangozzi" of Spoleto *and* "ciriole" of Terni, *and the equally delicious* "strascinati", "umbrici" (large, heavy noodles) *and of course various kinds of* risotto, *which are even more delicious, if accompanied by truffles. Completing the list are* "brodo di castrato" *(broth made from mutton) and* "acqua cotta" *(a soup made from bread, vegetables and eggs). Amongst the main courses, which are usually roasted on a spit, grilled or cooked in a wood oven, we find* roast-suckling pig *and* "intocco", roasted pork loin, grilled pork *and* lamb ribs *and* various offal dishes. *Fish dishes to be found include the excellent* "tegamaccio del Trasimeno" *(freshwater fish stew with white wine and herbs),* "regina in porchetta" *(Trasimeno carp cooked with herbs in a wood oven) and a wide range of fried fish dishes. A vast assortment of desserts and biscuits complete the broad spectrum of regional gastronomic dishes. Worthy of note are the* sweet Christmas gnocchi, pine-nut biscuits of Perugia, "ciaramicole" *(a ring-shaped pink cake covered with meringues and almond sweets),* "stinchetti" *(marzipan biscuits),* "cicerchiata" *(a ring-shaped cake made of small honey and cream puffs),* "pan nociato" of Todi *(a nut-flavoured cake), and* "serpentone delle cappuccine".

The production of wine in Umbria is an age old tradition: the full flavoured and robust wines produced in this ancient land were even familiar to the Romans. The wines of Umbria have always been synonymous with purity and simplicity. If the Orvieto bianco *(both the dry and "abboccato" variety) is considered to be the prince of Umbrian wines, other equally high quality wines (which are all subject to strict controls before being given the "DOC" - Certificate of Origin - label) are widely available for experts and connoisseurs, who wish to find a fitting accompaniment to the specialities of Umbrian cuisine. Wines worth tasting are* Torgiano *(white and red)*; Colli del Trasimeno *(white and red)*; Montefalco *(red and the robust* Sagrantino*)*; Colli Altotiberini DOC *(red, rosé and white)*; Colli Perugini *(red, rosé and white)*; Trebbiano dei Colli Martani and the Novello dei Colli Amerini.

Museum Opening Times

ASSISI - *Treasury Museum*, 9.30a.m.- 12.30p.m.; 2.30p.m.-5.00p.m., summer only, closed on Mondays.

ASSISI - *Municipal Picture Gallery*, 9.00a.m.-12.30p.m.; 3.00p.m. - 6.00p.m. (4.00p.m.-7.00p.m. in summer); Sundays and public holidays 9.00a.m. - 12.30p.m., closed on Mondays.

ASSISI - *Civic Museum*, 9.30a.m. - 12.30p.m.; 3.00p.m. - 7.00p.m.; Sundays and public holidays 9.00a.m. - 12.30p.m., closed on Mondays.

ASSISI - *Cathedral Museum*, 8.30a.m. - 1.00p.m.; 3.00p.m. - 6.00p.m.

BEVAGNA - *Municipal Picture Gallery*, 8.00a.m. - 2.00p.m.

CITTÀ DI CASTELLO - *Municipal Picture Gallery*, 9.00a.m. - 1.00p.m.; 3.00p.m. - 6.00.m., closed on Mondays.

CITTÀ DI CASTELLO - *Burri Museum*, 10.00a.m. - 12.00p.m.; 3.00p.m. - 5.00p.m., closed on Mondays.

FOLIGNO - *Picture Gallery*, 9.00a.m. - 1.00p.m.; 3.00p.m. - 7.00p.m (2.00p.m. - 4.00p.m. in winter); Sundays and public holidays 9.00a.m. - 2.00p.m.

GUBBIO - *Palazzo dei Consoli (Consuls'Palace)*, 9.00a.m. - 1.00p.m.; 3.00p.m. - 5.00p.m.(in summer, remains open until 7.00p.m.).

GUBBIO - *Palazzo Ducale (Ducal Palace)*, 9.00a.m. - 1.00p.m.; closed on Mondays.

MONTEFALCO - *Picture Gallery*, 10.00a.m. - 1.00p.m.; 3.30p.m. - 6.30p.m., closed on Thursdays.

NARNI - *Museum of St Dominic*, 8.00a.m. - 2.00p.m., closed on Sundays and public holidays.

NOCERA UMBRA - *Picture Gallery*, 8.00a.m. - 2.00p.m; 3.00p.m. - 7.00p.m.

ORVIETO - *Cathedral Museum*, 9.00a.m. - 12.00p.m.; 2.30p.m. - 4.30p.m.; (9.00a.m. - 1.00p.m; 3.00p.m. - 6.00p.m. in summer), closed on Mondays.

ORVIETO - *Civic Museum*, 9.00a.m. - 1.00p.m.; 3.00p.m. - 6.30p.m. (2.30p.m. - 4.30p.m. in winter).

ORVIETO - *Pozzo di San Patrizio (St Patrick's Well) and the Museum of E.Greco*, 9.00a.m. - 7.00p.m.

PERUGIA - *Cathedral Museum*, 9.00a.m. - 11.30a.m.; 3.30p.m. - 5.30p.m., closed on Mondays.

PERUGIA - *National Gallery of Umbria*, 9.00a.m. - 2.00p.m.; Public holidays and Sundays 9.00a.m. - 1.00p.m., closed on Mondays.

PERUGIA - *Sala del Collegio della Mercanzia (Merchants' Guilds Hall)*, 9.00a.m. - 12.30p.m.; 3.00p.m. - 6.00p.m.; Public holidays and Sundays 9.00a.m. - 12.30p.m., closed on Mondays.

PERUGIA - *Collegio del Cambio (The Old Exchange)*, 9.00a.m. - 12.30p.m.; 3.00p.m. - 5.00p.m.; Public holidays and Sundays 9.00a.m. - 12.30p.m., closed on Mondays.

PERUGIA - *National Archaeological Museum of Umbria*, 9.00a.m. - 1.30p.m.; Public holidays and Sundays 9.00a.m.-1.00p.m., closed on Mondays.

SPELLO - *Picture Gallery of S. Maria Maggiore*, 8.00a.m. - 12.00p.m.; 3.00p.m. - 6.00p.m.

SPOLETO - *Municipal Picture Gallery*, 9.00a.m. - 1.00p.m; 3.30p.m. - 5.30p.m.; (5.30p.m. - 8.00p.m. in summer), closed on Tuesdays.

SPOLETO - *Civic Museum*, 10.00a.m. - 1.00p.m.; 4.00p.m. - 6.00p.m. (10.00a.m. - 12.30p.m.; 4.00p.m. - 6.30p.m., in summer)

SPOLETO - *Gallery of Modern Art*, 10.00a.m. - 1.00p.m.; 3.00p.m. - 6.00p.m, closed on Tuesdays.

TERNI - *Picture Gallery and Archaeological Museum*, 9.00a.m. - 1.00p.m., closed on Mondays.

TREVI - *Picture Gallery*, 8.00a.m. - 2.00p.m.

Perugia, a panoramic view of the city

PERUGIA

HISTORICAL BACKGROUND - *The capital city of Umbria and of the Province (i.e. Province of Perugia), Perugia stretches out on a hilly ridge situated between the basin of Trasimeno and the Valtiberina. The city is extremely important in artistic, monumental and urban terms and is the seat of major cultural institutions. Prehistoric finds have provided proof of the existence of extremely ancient human settlements in the area. Herodotus Pliny and Dionysius of Halicarnassus made references to the founding of a proto-historic settlement by the Sarsinate Umbrians. Between the 6C and 5C BC. the Etruscans had penetrated most of the region of Umbria. Having become one of the twelve key cities of the Etruscan federation (4C-3C), it then went on to become a Roman colony after the epic battle of Sentino (295 BC.), which brought an end to its Etruscan domination. Allied to Rome during the Punic Wars, it became a place of refuge for the soldiers who survived the fatal battle which Rome lost at Trasimeno (217 BC.). After a period of relative calm and well-being, the city was involved in the Civil War between Octavian and Mark Anthony, whose brother Lucius tried in vain to resist the troops of Octavian. Having won the war, Octavian's troops then ravaged and sacked the city. Some years later, Octavian, by then Emperor Augustus, rebuilt the city and named it after himself* Augusta Perusia. *The city then passed into oblivion during the Imperial Age. The first Christian settlements appeared in the city around the 4C. During the Gothic War S.Ercolano (548 D.C.) was martyred here. It was controlled by the Byzantines for a long period before being subjected to ecclesiastical rule (8C). From the 11C onwards, the first free communes were set up. The 12C and 13C heralded a period of struggle and unrest, when Perugia fought against Chiusi, Cortona, Assisi, Todi and Foligno. After the city of Assisi was defeated at Collestrada (1202) Perugia extended its power and control over the Valdichiana and the Apennine ridges. Even in Perugia at the beginning of the 14C, disruptive elements came to the surface, engendered by the social structure of the city itself. The battles fought out between the Raspanti (the wealthy merchant class) and Beccherini nobles, as well as the never ending struggles between the most important local "bigwigs" (Vincioli, Montesperelli, Montemelini, Della Corgna, Baglioni, Oddi) led to the town being subjected to the Church. During the period of noble rule, several individuals rose to power, including Biordo Michelotti, Braccio Fortebraccio, Niccolò Piccinino and Braccio Baglioni. Meanwhile the weakening of the commune's structure led to the disintegration of the social and economic fabric of the city. After the vain expectations of liberty created by Napoleon, the city factions became a united front in the battles for the national "Risorgimento", during which the abhorred Papal fortress (built as a symbol of Papal absolutism) was destroyed, and the Swiss Guards were thrown out of the town. As a result, the city became a part of the Kingdom of Italy (1860).*

13

Perugia, the magnificent Priors' Palace and a detail of the portal in the façade, with bronze statues of a Griffin and a Lion

PRIORS' PALACE - Also known as the *Town Hall,* the building is an outstanding example of medieval architecture and is considered to be amongst the most elegant and famous in Italy. Begun by Giacomo di Servadio and Giovannello di Benvenuto (1293), it was completed in 1443, when further additions, in the form of houses and pre-existing towers, were all combined under one huge roof. The main **façade** facing out over *Corso Vannucci,* has breathtaking proportions; it is surmounted by a Tower, which was reduced in height in the second half of the 16C. The building also has a wealth of mullioned windows with three and four lights. The splendid round **portal** resembles those found in cathedrals, as it is rich in ornamental decorations. The splayed portal has friezes, twisted columns, sculptures and ornamental foliage. The beautiful lunette contains the figures of *St Laurence, S.Lodovico of Tolosa* and *S.Ercolano.* The **façade** looking out over *Piazza IV November* has a flight of steps leading up to a pointed portal. On the left side is a loggia containing a pulpit. Above the portal are bronze statues of a *Griffin* (the symbol of the city) and a *Lion* (symbol of the Guelphs), which constitute the first attempts at large-scale casting made in 13C Italy. Above are five mullioned windows with three lights. The whole building is crowned by Guelph merlons. The **Atrium** (entrance-hall) is a covered courtyard with pillars and vaults, from which a large staircase leads up to the **Sala dei Notari** (the lawyers' meeting hall). The imposing medieval hall with grandiose arches has frescoed vaults depicting *Scenes from the Bible* and episodes from *Aesop's Fables.* These frescoes were painted by pupils of P. Cavallini (13C-14C). On the walls are the coats of arms of the Podestà and Captains of the People. Other rooms in the building include the **Sala del Consiglio Comunale** (the Hall of the City Council) (containing a fresco by Pinturicchio) and the **Sala Rossa** (the Red Hall) (containing a mural by Dono Doni of Perugia).

Perugia, a view of the interior and details of the elaborate decorative sculptures which enhance the magnificent Priors' Palace

Perugia, National Gallery of Umbria: S. Maria dei Fossi by Pinturicchio

THE NATIONAL GALLERY OF UMBRIA - The gallery is situated on the third floor of the Priors' Palace and contains masterly examples of the paintings of the Umbrian school, which date from the 13C to the 19C. The **Sala Maggiore** (Great Hall) contains detached frescoes (12C-15C) and a wooden *Deposition* dating from the 13C; **Room 1**: *Madonna and Child* by Duccio di Buoninsegna; *Crucifixion* by Maestro di S.Francesco. **Room 2**: reliefs originating from a town fountain by A. di Cambio. **Rooms 3-4**: works of the Siennese and Perugian schools; *Crucifixion* (stained glass) by G. di Bonino; *Saints*, a panel attributed to Francesco da Rimini. **Room 5**: paintings of the Siennese school (14C-15C); bronze *Lion* and *Griffins* (formerly located at the Great Fountain). **Room 6**: Late Gothic and International Gothic paintings; *Madonna and Child* by Gentile da Fabriano. **Room 7**: Renaissance paintings, a triptych by Fra Angelico and a polyptych by Piero della Francesca. **Rooms 8-9**: paintings by artists from the Marches and works by the Umbrian School; works by B. Bonfigli, G. Boccati, B. Caporali, F. di Lorenzo. **Room 10**: works by Antoniazzo Romano, Giuliano da Cremona and others. **Room 11**: *Adoration of the Shepherds* by Fiorenzo di Lorenzo. **Rooms 12-13**: *Adoration of the Magi*, by Perugino; *Miracles of S. Bernardino* (Pinturicchio, Perugino and probably Bramante). **Room 14**: *The Dead Christ* by Perugino; *S.Maria dei Fossi* by Pinturicchio. **Rooms 15-21**: paintings dating from the first half of the 16C; paintings by Alfani and Doni. **Room 22**: gold jewellery, ivory objects and bronzes. **Room 23 (Priors' Chapel)**: frescoes by Bonfigli. **Room 24**: sculptures by Agostino di Duccio. **Room 25**: 13C-15C detached frescoes. **Rooms 26-33**: Mannerist paintings and works dating from the beginning of the 17C; handicrafts;

maps; ancient Perugian tablecloths; works by A. Fiammingo, O. Gentileschi, P. da Cortona and A. Sacchi.

COLLEGIO DELLA MERCANZIA (MERCHANTS' GUILDS HALL) - The entrance to the building is situated in *Corso Vannucci*. The walls and vaults of this rectangular room are decorated with 15C inlaid wooden panelling. The counter was splendidly carved by Costanzo di Mattiolo, a 15C local artist.

COLLEGIO DEL CAMBIO (THE OLD EXCHANGE) - Situated next to the Priors' Palace, at the end of the Via dei Priori, the building contains superlative works of Renaissance art. The **Sala dei Legisti** (the Hall of the Jurists) contains beautiful counters with valuable 17C carvings by G. Zuccari. The **Sala dell'Udienza del Cambio** (the Hall of the Exchange Sessions) is decorated with wonderful frescoes by the most famous Umbrian painters. Here, Pietro Vannucci, better known as "Perugino" developed his artistic qualities along with Raphael and Andrea d'Assisi. The subjects depicted in the frescoes include *Historical Characters and Philosophers*, *Cardinal Virtues*, a *self-portrait* and *Religious Scenes, Prophets* and *Sibyls*. The annexed **Chapel of St John the Baptist** contains frescoes by Gian Nicola di Paolo (16C).

CATHEDRAL OF ST LAURENCE - This imposing Gothic temple was constructed between the 14C and 15C, although a large amount of its external facing remains incomplete. The simple, coarse stone **façade** has a massive Baroque portal by P. Carattoli (first half of the 18C). In the upper part of the façade is an enormous oculus. The **left side** of the building, which looks out over the central *Piazza IV Novembre* is decorated by a portal built by Alessi with ornamental masks by Scalza. Above

Perugia, the spectacular Fontana Maggiore which stands opposite the side of the Cathedral

the portal is a votive *Crucifix*, placed here by the people of Perugia in 1539. On one side of the portal is the pulpit of S. Bernardino (15C). On the other side of the portal, on top of a flight of steps, stands the *Statue of Pope Julius III*, a masterly bronze work by V. Danti (16C). The **interior**, which is divided into a nave and two aisles by robust octagonal pillars, has the appearance of a large hall of harmonious proportions. The cross vaults contain 18C frescoes. On the right is the *Tomb of Andrea Baglioni* by Urbano da Cortona. The **Chapel of S.Bernardino**, which is enclosed by beautiful wrought iron railings, contains a 16C fresco by Federico Barocci depicting the *Deposition*, generally believed to be the master-piece of this Umbrian artist. Also to be seen are the multicoloured stained glass window by Arrigo Fiammingo (16C) and 16C pews by Jacopo Fiorentino and Ercole di Tommaso. The stained glass window and all the frescoes in the **Chapel of the Baptistery** are by Domenico Bruschi (19C). Along the nave (third pillar) is the venerated image of the *Madonna of the Graces,* by Giannicola di Paolo, a pupil of Pietro Vannucci. The **Chapel of the Sacrament** designed by Alessi has late 18C frescoes by Marcello Leopardi. In the right transept are the *Tombs of Pope Martin IV, Pope Urban IV and Pope Innocenzo III* and the marble sculpture dedicated to *Pope Leo XIII* (19C). The presbytery is illuminated by modern stained glass windows and contains beautifully carved choir stalls by Giuliano da Maiano and Domenico del Tasso (15C). Here too are two 15C lecterns and a bishop's throne. A beautiful 16C wooden *Crucifix* decorates the altar of the left transept. The walls of the left aisle contain fragments of a sculptured altar-frontal by A. di Antonio di Duccio and Benedetto Baglioni. The altar of the banner is decorated with a 16C processional standard, by Berto di Giovanni. The **Chapel of the Holy Ring**, enclosed by beautiful wrought iron railings (15C), is lit by a modern stained glass window. Within the chapel is a silver and gold plated copper tabernacle, a masterly 16C piece of engraving by Federico di Francesco and Bino di Pietro. This contains the holy relic of an onyx wedding ring, which is supposed to have been worn by the Virgin Mary. Also to be seen is the *Tomb of Marcantonio Oddi*, a 17C work by Domenico Guidi. The **Sacristy** contains ancient furnishings and inlaid work by Mariotto di Paolo (15C). The walls have frescoes depicting the *Stories from the Bible, Figures of Popes* and *Doctors of the Church* (G. A. Pandolfi 16C).

CATHEDRAL MUSEUM - One enters the museum through the Cathedral cloister. The museum contains furnishings, vestments, painted panels and works, which were once contained in the Cathedral itself. There is also a collection of rare miniatures and paintings. Worthy of note is the *Madonna Enthroned with Saints* by Luca Signorelli; a *Pietà* by B. Caporali; the *Virgin and Saints* by Meo di Guido da Siena.

CIVIC MUSEUM OF NATURAL HISTORY - The museum is located in the **Bishops' Palace**. The exhibits on show in the museum were originally collected by Pope Leo XIII (the Bishop of Perugia for over thirty years) who in turn donated his private collections to the city. A large range of exhibits from the animal, vegetable and plant world can be seen.

LOGGIAS OF BRACCIO FORTEBRACCIO - An outstanding example of Renaissance architecture (15C), the loggias are all that remain of an ancient palace built by Braccio (Fortebraccio), a famous "condottiere" (military leader), who took control of the city during the period of noble domination. The loggias were built by Fioravante Fioravanti of Bologna. They are situated at the beginning of the street named *Via delle Volte.*

FONTANA MAGGIORE (THE GREAT FOUNTAIN) - The fountain stands in the central *Piazza IV Novembre,* the main tourist attraction and monumental heart of medieval Perugia. Looking out over the square are the Priors' Palace, the Bishop's Palace and the Lawyers' Meeting Hall (Palazzo dei Notari), the side of the Cathedral and the Loggias of Braccio Fortebraccio. The fountain was built in 1275-78 and designed by Fra' Bevignate, assisted by Boninsegna da Venezia. The marble decorative sculptures were carved by Nicola and Giovanni Pisano, who also built the three bronze *Water Carriers.* The casting of the top bronze basin and column is attributed to Rosso Padellaio of Perugia. The upper stone basin, sustained by small columns with capitals, consists of 24 red marble panels separated by 24 statues. The bas-reliefs represent *Views,*

Perugia, a view of the Basilica of St Domenic, and the two buttresses which characterize the façade

Historical events, Scenes from the Bible, Historical and mythological figures, Allegorical representations of religious and theological subjects, Saints. The lower basin has 50 panels, on which are depicted the *Months of the Year,* the *Signs of the Zodiac, Liberal arts, Scenes from the Old Testament, The Founding of Rome, Aesop's Fables.*

CORSO VANNUCCI - The central thoroughfare of Perugia, lined with austere and imposing buildings of great architectural merit, is the street along which residents and numerous tourists traditionally take their evening stroll. As well as the Priors' Palace, the Collegio del Cambio and the Collegio della Mercanzia (Merchants' Guilds Hall), other buildings along this street include the **Palazzo dei Notari** (Lawyers' Meeting Hall) (15C), a beautiful Renaissance building; the **House of Baldo degli Ubaldi** (15C), at the beginning of *Via Baldo;* the 16C **Church of S.Isidoro** by G. Danti (de-consecrated) in *Piazza della Repubblica;* the frescoed **Donini Palace** (dates from 1716). Further along, the Corso leads to *Piazza Italia,* constructed upon the bastions of the ruined **Paolina Fortress**.

THE CHURCH OF S. ERCOLANO - The church, which is dedicated to the patron saint of Perugia, stands on the spot where S.Ercolano was martyred by Totila, during the period when the Goths besieged the city (547). The Gothic building, built between the 13C and the 14C, has an octagonal plan and is characterized by slender, large pointed arches, with a series of small blind arches under the upper cornice. One enters the **interior** by means of a beautiful double staircase (1607). The upper Baroque additions serve, if nothing else, to highlight the beauty of the original medieval features. On the high altar, a noteworthy Roman sarcophagus (3C) contains the mortal remains of the patron saint. The cupola has frescoes painted by Giuli and Carlone.

MARZIA GATE - The gate is situated in the encirclement of the external walls of the **Paolina Fortress**. It was transferred from its original site by Sangallo, during the period when the Fortress was constructed. It is a superb example of Etruscan architecture (3C BC.) and is decorated with *Reliefs of Equestrian Heads* and with *Virile Figures.*

NATIONAL ARCHAEOLOGICAL MUSEUM OF UMBRIA - The museum is located in the Cloister of the former monastery of St Domenic. The museum contains Etruscan and Roman epigraphs, urns, sarcophagi and other exhibits discovered in the tombs and subterranean tombs in the district of Perugia and the immediate vicinity. The prehistoric section includes exhibits dating from the Palaeolithic, Bronze and Iron ages, which come from Central Italy and other parts of the world. Amongst the most interesting finds in the Etruscan-Roman section are the burial apparel discovered in the necropolises of Perugia (Frontone, Monteluce, St Catherine, S.Giuliana, Sperandio); the stela (ancient pillar) of Mt

Perugia, the interior of the Church of St Peter

Gualandro; the Cippus (or memorial stone) of Perugia; the chariot of Castel S.Mariano. The museum also contains important exhibits found in other Etruscan sites of Umbria.

BASILICA OF ST DOMENIC - The imposing Gothic construction (14C) was rebuilt by Carlo Maderno in the first half of the 17C. On either side of the bare **façade** are buttresses, which continue around to the sides of the church. An elegant late 16C portal and a double flight of steps decorate the façade. The enormous stark **interior** of the church contains side chapels. The fourth chapel on the right is part of the original building and contains a painted arch by A.di Antonio di Duccio. The transept chapel contains many votive frescoes. Works of art include an 18C organ; the *Tomb of Elisabetta Cantucci,* carved by Algardi; the *Tomb of the Danti family;* the splendid *Tomb of Pope Benedict XI,* the work of a pupil of Arnolfo di Cambio. The apse is lit by a large window, beautifully decorated by Fra' Bartolomeo di Pietro and Mariotto di Nardo (15C). The 15C inlaid wooden choir is the work of Crispolto da Bettona and Antonio da Mercatello. Moving towards the entrance, the first chapel on the right is part of the original church and is decorated with 14C frescoes influenced by the Siennese school. At the altar of the third chapel is a painted banner, depicting *Perugia at the beginning of the 16C.* The **Sacristy** contains some sacred vestments belonging to Pope Benedict XI.

GATE OF ST PETER - This construction is in fact made up of two gates: the one facing *Corso Cavour* dates from the 14C, while the other is a masterly example of Renaissance architecture, based on the Malatesta Temple at Rimini. It is the work of Agostino di Antonio di Duccio (15C).

BASILICA OF ST PETER - In front of the building is an elegant courtyard lined with arches, into which one enters by means of a 17C loggia. The building is dominated by a beautiful **Bell tower**, which has an elevated spire and is exquisitely decorated by mullioned windows with two lights situated above a series of large jutting corbels, which resemble a cornice; it was built to a design by Rossellino and completed by Giovanni di Betto and Puccio di Paolo in the 15C. The **interior** of the basilica is divided into a nave and two aisles by 18 Roman columns from the original church. The wealth of art works which decorate the church contribute to the atmosphere of majestic solemnity, which pervades the interior. The church, built in the 10C on the site of the ancient cathedral, has a lacunar ceiling over the central nave by Benedetto di Montepulciano (16C). There are ten large canvases by Aliense (Antonio Vassilacchi), depicting *Scenes from the Old and New Testaments* decorating the nave. On the counter-façade is an imposing painting of the *Benedict Order;* at the sides of the portal are the *Scenes from the Lives of St Peter and St Paul* (O. Alfani, L Cungi). The walls of the presbytery contain frescoes by S. Pecennini, B. Bandiera, G. Fiammingo and Giambattista della Marca. Also to be seen is the masterly high altar by V. Martelli (17C), the carved pews by Benedetto de Montepulciano and Benvenuto da Brescia, and the choir, one of the most beautiful in Italy, the work of a considerable number of 16C artists. In the **Sacristy** are works by Perugino, Caravaggio and Algardi, as well as some 15C furnishings. In the left aisle, moving towards the entrance, is a *Pieta* (B Bonfigli); the **Vibi Chapel** (containing a fine marble tabernacle by Mino da Fiesole); the **Ranieri Chapel** (with paintings by G. Reni); the **Chapel of the Sacrament** (containing pictures by Vasari) and finally a *Pieta* by Perugino. The annexed convent, which has been taken over by the University, contain a beautiful **Large Cloister** with an architrave over the portal (16C); the **Refectory** contains a terracotta wash-basin by Benedetto Buglione, a pupil of the Della Robbias (15C) and the **Star Cloister** (16C) built to designs by Alessi.

FRONTONE GARDEN - This public garden, once owned by Fortebraccio and the Baglioni family, contains an **Amphitheatre** dating from the second half of the 18C, designed by Baldassare Orsini. Nearby, beyond **The Gate of S. Costanzo** (16C) stands the **Church** bearing the same name. This is a pretty Neo-Byzantine building designed by Calderini (19C).

THE CHURCH OF ST GIULIANA - Built in the 13C, the Church is characterized by a beautiful **Bell tower** with a spire. The **façade**, exquisitely decorated with multicoloured marble, contains a portal and an elaborate rose window., The **interior**, which is simple and elegant, has wooden cross beams and contains 13C-14C frescoes, many of which are detached. The annexed 14C **Cloister**, believed to be the work of Gattapone, has a double portico and is of great architectural interest.

VIA DEI PRIORI - An enchanting section of medieval Perugia, with many interesting buildings contained both in the street itself and in the immediate vicinity. The **Church of St Agatha** dating from the 13C contains 14C frescoes. In the vicinity is the ex-**Oratory of the Majesty of the Vaults**, with a painting of the *Madonna and Child* attributed to the 14C "Maestro delle Volte" (lit. Master of the Vaults). The 13C **Sciri Tower** is one of the few surviving towers (once there were over 70) of medieval Perugia. At the end of the street is the **Trasimeno Gate** or the *Arch of St Luke*, an Etruscan construction, reconstructed in medieval times. Nearby stands the **Church of the Madonna della Luce** (lit. of the Light), which is a beautiful Renaissance construction.

THE CHURCH OF S. FILIPPO NERI - A marvellous example of Baroque architecture, the church has an extremely elaborate **façade** in two orders, designed by P. Marucelli (17C). The **interior** has a nave and contains side chapels. Numerous paintings and 18C frescoes decorate the church. At the high altar is an *Assumption* by Pietro da Cortona (17C).

Perugia, the Renaissance façade of the Oratory of S. Bernardino, and the façade of the Church of S. Francesco al Prato (13C)

THE CHURCH OF S. PROSPERO - This place of worship, which is incorporated in a farm building is extremely ancient, probably dating back to the Early Christian period and is built over an Etruscan tomb. The **interior** contains an extremely valuable early medieval ciborium(8C). A side chapel has a cycle of frescoes by the Perugian painter Bonamico (1225) which are quite exceptional, as the date and signature of the artist can be clearly made out.

ORATORY OF S. BERNARDINO - The date of completion (1461) can be seen in the inscription situated on the frieze below the tympanum dominating the **façade**. The building is the masterly work of the Florentine architect and sculptor Agostino di Antonio di Duccio and clearly shows the maturity gained by the artist as a result of working alongside Leon Battista Alberti (Rimini, Malatesta Temple). A wonderful cycle of sculptures, depicting *Saints* and *Celestial Hierarchies,* and the *Glory of S.Bernardino* are important examples of the Perugia-Renaissance style. The 15C interior, in the Gothic style, contains (on the high altar) the *Tomb of Beato Egidio*, a Roman sarcophagus (4C AD.). By going through the annexed **Oratory of St Andrew** (16C) which is a Neo-classical building, and the sacristy of the oratory, one enters the Baldeschi Chapel, where Bartolo da Sassoferrato, a famous 14C jurist and a teacher at the General "Studium" of Perugia, is buried.

THE CHURCH OF S. FRANCESCO AL PRATO - An imposing 13C construction, which has an outstanding **façade** flanked by two turreted towers. The influence of the Cosmatesque sculptors is clearly visible. Various elements and features combine together to create an exquisite mosaic: square tiles, diamond shapes and small marble panels all blend in perfectly with the geometric proportions of the façade, which is crowned by a triangular tympanum and superbly decorated with small arches, a rose window and an elegant portal. At present., large scale reconstruction work is being carried out in the **interior**, which nowadays, therefore, has the appearance of a large, partly covered, empty hall. From the left side of the building, decorated by a central portal and a mullioned window with two lights, one enters the **Chapel of the Banner**, once known as the *Oddi Chapel*. This building contains a painted banner depicting the *Madonna della Mercede* (lit. reward) by Bonfigli (15C). In the Chapel, the famous "condottiere" Braccio Fortebraccio is buried.

THE UNIVERSITY FOR FOREIGNERS - The building, which looks out over *Piazza Fortebraccio* was once known as the *Antinori Palace* and then later on as the *Gallenga Stuart Palace.* The University is an imposing Rococo construction in three orders and is decorated by pillars. It was built in 1758 by Pietro Carattoli, to plans by the architect Bianchi.

ETRUSCAN ARCH - Otherwise known as the *Arch of Augustus,* the original construction dates from the 3C-2C BC. and incorporates later Roman and 16C additions. The gate is situated between two robust Etruscan towers; the one on the right has been lowered, while the one on the left has a beautiful fountain (1621) decorating its base and a 16C portico on its upper part. Above the gate is a sentinel arch, which has now been walled up.

THE CHURCH OF ST AUGUSTINE - This fine construction dates from the 13C. The extremely elegant **façade** (which has undergone many transformations) is decorated by geometrical motifs in the upper order, while the lower order is adorned with small white and red square tiles and the wonderful double portal. The **interior**, which was restructured at the turn of the 18C, contains some Gothic and Renaissance chapels. The beautiful choir in the apse is a masterly work by Baccio d'Agnolo, based on drawings by Perugino. The adjacent **Oratory of the Brotherhood of St Augustine** dates from 1415; the building contains a beautiful carved gilt ceiling (17C).

TEMPLE OF ST MICHAEL THE ARCHANGEL - A charming Early Christian construction dating back to the 5C. The circular shaped temple was constructed with building materials taken from ancient pagan buildings. The central lantern rests on 16 Roman marble columns. The altar has been carved out of a shaft of a column with a marble slab dating from the Roman period. The church is more simply known as the *Church of S.Angelo*.

Perugia, a view of the so-called Etruscan Arch set in the mighty walls, and a charming view of the Temple of St Michael the Archangel

CAPTAIN OF THE PEOPLE'S PALACE - A masterly Renaissance construction attributed to Gasparino d'Antonio and Leone di Matteo (15C), the building looks out over *Piazza Matteotti,* along which is also situated the 15C **Old University Building**. The beautiful **façade**, which once had a second order decorated with mullioned windows with three lights and surmounted by merlons, is embellished by a fine portal adorned with *Griffins* and a fresco of *Justice* in the lunette. On the first floor are graceful mullioned windows with two lights and the loggia of the town crier, sustained by large ornate corbels.

THE CHURCH OF JESUS - The construction dates from the second half of the 16C and is the result of an ingenious architectural solution, whereby the difference in the varying heights of three buildings was compensated for by the construction of an underlying road. The present day **façade** in the Neo-classical style, has two orders decorated by pilaster strips and is crowned by triangular tympanum. The building was completed with the aid of a painting dating from the period of the original construction. In the **interior**, which was damaged in a fire on the 30th January 1989, are 17C frescoes by Giovanni Andrea Carlone, depicting *Episodes from the Life of Giosuè*. Unfortunately, the remarkable wooden ceiling, which had beautiful decorations and carvings, was burnt in the fire.

THE CHURCH OF S.FIORENZO - The present building is the result of 18C remoulding work carried out by Carattoli on the original Gothic building. In the **interior** is a 15C votive banner, painted by Bonfigli. Once the church contained a masterly *Madonna degli Ansidei* by Raffaello Sanzio, which has now been transferred to London.

THE CHURCH OF S. SEVERO - The church was first built (at the beginning of the 11C) on a sacred pagan site, consecrated to the God of the Sun, upon which there once stood a temple. The present building is the result of reconstruction work carried out in the 18C. In the annexed **Oratory** is a masterly fresco by Raphael (*Trinity and Saints,* 1505) to which Perugino added the *Figures of Saints* (1521) after the death of the great painter from Urbino.

THE CHURCH OF S. MARIA NUOVA - The 13C building has been reconstructed many times. It also includes a **Cloister**, which is dominated by a beautiful 17C **Bell tower** built to plans by Alessi. The **interior** contains Renaissance features, while the aisles and the apse still betray Gothic features. The beautiful carved wooden choir is a 15C work by Paolino di Giovanni and Giovanni da Montelparo. There is also a 15C painted banner by Bonfigli and the 90 terricolous (above ground) tombs of the ancient "Clerici Vagantes" (lit. wandering clerics).

THE CHURCH OF S. MARIA DI MONTELUCE - Constructed in the 13C, the Church has a beautiful **façade** decorated by small white and red square tiles, a large rose window and a double portal. At the side of the façade is an aedicule, located at the base of an imposing bell tower, which remains incomplete. The **interior** has one nave and contains 17C reconstruction work. However, one can still admire the marble high altar (14C), the 15C tabernacle by Francesco Ferrucci da Fiesole and a copy of the *Coronation of the Virgin* by Giulio Romano, based on a drawing by Raphael, painted by Giovanni Silvagni (19C).

THE CHURCH OF S. BEVIGNATE - This 13C building has a simple **façade** flanked by two imposing buttresses. The Romanesque portal is surmounted by a large oculus. The **interior** contains a wealth of frescoes by local artists dating from the end of the 13C. The most outstanding ones are those on the counter-façade (*Knights in Battle)* and those decorating the apse (*Universal Judgement).*

Amongst the other features of interest in Perugia, mention should also be made of the **Arco della Mandorla** (lit. the Almond Arch), an ancient Etruscan gate, the original arch of which was modified to a pointed one in the 13C, and a **Roman Mosaic** dating from the 2C AD. The mosaic, situated under the portico of the Chemistry Department of the University (*via Pascoli*) is all that remains of an ancient spa building. The small black and white tesserae depict *Orpheus soothing the wild animals with*

Sunset over Acquasparta

his lyre. Recent excavation work in via Caporali (1989) has also unearthed an **Etruscan Cistern** dating back to the mid 3C BC. This, together with the 3C **Sorbello Well** in *Piazza Piccinino,* are important examples of hydraulic engineering systems of the Etruscan period.

ENVIRONS - A little outside Perugia at the **Bridge of St John** is the **Tomb of the Volumni**. The tomb is one of the most famous Etruscan subterranean tombs in Umbria. It dates back to between the 3C and the 2C BC. The **Tomb of Villa Sperandio** is located outside the Gate of S. Angelo. In the vaulted chamber, carved deeply into the tufa rock, is a travertine sarcophagus. The **Tomb of S.Manno** is located near the village of S.Manno, in the courtyard of an ancient fortified monastery. The subterranean tomb, which is well preserved, is an important example of funerary architecture of the 3C BC. and forms the crypt of a Romanesque church. A little outside the playing fields of the **Plain of Massiano**, on a sunny green hill situated in a splendid panoramic position looking out towards Perugia, stands **Spagnolia** the *Città della Domenica* (the *Sunday City).*

ACQUASPARTA

From its hill-top position, the well-known spa town of Acquasparta, in the province of Terni, faces the Martani mountains and looks down over the Via Flaminia which runs through the underlying valley of the Naia. The Romans enjoyed the curative powers of its waters and were in fact responsible for its development as a *pagus.* In medieval times, the town became a stronghold and was ruled by the Lombard Dukes of Spoleto. The medieval features of Acquasparta have been perfectly preserved within the **town walls**, upon which stand circular towers.
Worth seeing is the Renaissance **Cesi Palace**, built in the second half of the 16C and designed by Giovanni Domenico de' Bianchi from Milan. The building, which was once the home of Cardinal Federico Cesi and the seat of the "Accademia dei Lincei", today belongs to the University of Perugia. Nearby stands the **Church of St Cecily** which contains a 16C chapel. Inside the church is the *tomb of Federico Cesi,* a 17th botanist. The **Church of St Francis** dates from the second half of the 13C and contains a beautiful 14C wooden *Crucifix*, an effigy of the *Virgin and Child*, and a copy of a painting by Margaritone d'Arezzo, depicting *Scenes from the life of St Francis.* Near the **Ancient Gate** contained within the town walls, alongside a beautiful round tower, stands the 17C **Church of the Madonna of the Lily.** The **Springs of Amerino**, once known as the *Springs of St Francis* contain an alkaline-bicarbonate water, which has a medium mineral content, like that found at the **Furapane Springs**, situated just outside the town.

ALVIANO

A typical, small, ancient town of the region, situated on a hill which is heavily cultivated and eroded by ravines. The mighty square fortress keeps vigil over the town. Alviano dominates that part of the valley where the Tiber has been dammed up to form an artificial lake, creating an interesting oasis for wild life. This area is considered to be one of the most characteristic marshlands in Umbria. The origins of the present place name seem to date back to Roman times, when it was inhabited by the *Gens Albia*. In the area, which is characterized by a rural economy, some interesting folk festivals are held, such as the *"Cantata della Vecchiarella"* (night of Epiphany) and a re-enactment of the *Passion of Christ* (the evening of Good Friday). The most interesting tourist feature is the **Fortress**, an imposing square building, with round corner towers. The castle we see today is the result of restructuring work carried out by Bartolomeo d'Alviano (end of the 15C). An interesting *Museum of Rural Life* is situated in the large vaulted rooms on the ground floor. Also situated on the same floor is the *Centre of Audio-visual Documentation on the Oasis*, where natural history material of great interest can be seen. The first floor houses the offices of the local town council. In the *Chapel of St Francis* is a fresco depicting *The Miracle of the Saint*. The **Parish Church** dates from the 15C. The nave and two aisles of the interior are separated by columns, and a notable *Transfiguration of the Virgin* by Niccolò Alunno can be seen. In the right aisle is a fresco by Pordenone. Evidence of the past can frequently be found in the surrounding districts, such as at **Popiliano**, where archaeological remains have been uncovered. These include pieces of mosaic floors and coins which are believed to have originated from the **Villa of Popilio** (1C BC.)

AMELIA

Amelia is the largest town of the Amerino and is beautifully located on a hilly ridge between the Tiber and Nera valleys. Believed to be the oldest town in Umbria (some claim it was founded by Ameroe twelve centuries before Christ), Ameria was an Umbrian-Italic settlement, and it would not be hazarding too much of a guess to say that the first human settlements were established here between the 10C and the 11C BC. Having become a *Municipium* (90 BC.) and known as *Ameria*, it was later developed as a river port. Of great interest, due to their mighty structure and their considerable length, are the **polygonal walls**, which completely enclose the town; the oldest parts, dating back to between the 6C and 5C BC., were used to defend the acropolis. The **Cathedral**, first built in the Romanesque style, was later re-built in the 17C, after a fire had destroyed the original building. The interior, with a Latin cross-shaped plan, contains

View of the ancient town of Amelia

View over the picturesque roof-tops of Amelia

nineteenth century frescoes by Luigi Fontana. At the side of the Cathedral stands the **Civic Tower** (11C), an imposing twelve-sided Romanesque construction. **The Church of St Francis** has a delightful Romanesque-Gothic façade, a beautiful rose window and a fine portal. The building, once dedicated to *St James and St Philip*, has ancient 12C origins. Other places of worship include the **Church of St Augustine**. Also known as the *Church of St Pancras* (or of *St Mary of the Elm*), this is a 14C construction with Romanesque-Gothic motifs, a beautiful portal decorated. **The Farrattini Palace** was built in the first half of the 16C and designed by Antonio da Sangallo the Younger, who was inspired by the Farnese Palace in Rome. The building, which has simple and yet striking Renaissance features, has a Latin inscription in the façade commemorating Cardinal Bartolomeo Farrattini. The **Petrignani Palace** is also a 16C building and is decorated by windows dating from the same period, built from remains removed from a former ancient building. The rooms in the interior are decorated with paintings executed by pupils of the Zuccari brothers. Amongst the other palaces in the town, the **Town Hall** is worth visiting. Its courtyard contains archaeological exhibits dating back to the Roman Age. Whilst on this subject, it should be pointed out that over the last ten years considerable remains of Roman settlements in the area have been discovered in the environs of Amelia. These consist mainly of villas dating back to the 1C and 4C AD. Amongst the most important finds made at Amelia is the so-called *Colossus of Amelia*, a bronze sculpture of the Imperial Age, an astonishing work, both as regards its size (over 2.20m) and its artistic value. The work, which most probably represents *Germanicus*, son of Drusus the Elder, was discovered in the early 1960s. The **Social Theatre** dates from the second half of the 18C and is characterized by its horseshoe plan, a feature of the "theatres of light opera". Other interesting features of Amelia include the ancient **Loggia of the Town Criers** in *Piazza Marconi*, where the herald proclaimed the edicts of the commune, and the **Roman** (16C-17C), **Lion** (with enchanting medieval features) and **Posterula** (13C) town gates.

ARRONE

Picturesque village with a decidedly medieval configuration, Arrone lies on a green hill dominating the Nera valley, in an area characterized by woody reliefs. During medieval times, its strategically important position controlled the access to the valley along the important main thoroughfare which ensured links between Abruzzo and the Duchy of Spoleto.

In the oldest part of the village, known as *La Terra* (lit. the ground), one comes across the **Fortress** - a typical example of medieval architecture. Also in the Terra quarter can be seen the **Church of St John**, a Gothic construction dating from the 13C and 14C, which is characterized by a polygonal apse. In the interior, there are 15C votive frescoes along the walls, while the frescoes of the Umbrian school, dating from the same period, decorate the apse. These latter works show the strong influence of Piero della Francesca.

The **Church of St Mary**, built originally in the 13C, was enlarged in the 16C. The fine 15C portal and the frescoes decorating the apse are also interesting features. These frescoes were painted by Vincenzo Tamagni and Giovanni Brunotti in 1516 and depict the *Nativity*, the *Crowning of the Virgin* and the *Passing away of Our Lady*. Also to be seen are paintings by the pupils of Spagna.

The medieval village of Arrone, set along the wooded hillside

Assisi, a view of the city: in the foreground stands the robust medieval Basilica of St Francis

ASSISI

HISTORICAL BACKGROUND - *Beautifully situated on a fertile hill brightened up by olive groves and cypress trees, Assisi stretches out along the slopes of Mount Subasio in a lovely spot along that part of the Valle Umbra situated between the Tescio, Topino and Chiascio rivers. Originally an Umbrian settlement, the city developed along with other territories controlled by the Etruscans, under whose influence it prospered. Under Roman domination it was known as* Asisium. *Having become a flourishing* Municipium, *it was evangelized by the martyr Rufino (3C). With the fall of the Roman Empire, it was subjected to Barbarian invasions; destroyed by the Goths (545), it was then conquered by the Byzantines and afterwards fell into the hands of the Lombards. Incorporated into the territories controlled by the Duchy of Spoleto, it then became a free commune from the 11C onwards, achieving its greatest period of prosperity in the 13C. After a period of war and strife, it was besieged and conquered by Barbarossa (1174) who resided here three years later. Frederick II of Swabia was baptized here, but more importantly, Assisi is the birthplace of two people who have influenced both the history of the city and humanity itself: St Francis (1182) and St Clare (1193). Later the city was ruled in turn by the popes, Perugia, the Visconti family of Milan, the Montefeltro family and Braccio Fortebraccio, before finally coming under the control of the Sforza dynasty. Profoundly influenced by the internal struggles between the Nepis (of the upper town) and the Fiumi (of the lower town) factions, Assisi was then firmly established as a Papal possession from the 16C onwards. Modern-day Assisi has the characteristic configuration of a medieval town which is still encompassed within its ancient town walls. An extremely interesting centre for art and culture, it is also a religious hub of world-wide fame, and attracts pilgrims and tourists from all corners of the globe. The city streets the bright pinkish stone of Subasio which distinguishes its buildings, the religious intimacy which emanates from its most sacred corners, are all elements that make Assisi an undoubtedly fascinating place for visitors. In the city, which is also quite a popular spa resort, numerous traditional events are held throughout the year. Apart from the usual traditional events, religious festivals such as the* Festival of the Vows (22 June), the Festival of the Pardon *(1st/2nd August) and the* Festival of St Francis, Patron Saint of Italy *(3rd/4th October) are held every year. Amongst the traditional folk festivals are the famous* Calendimaggio (*a May Day celebration with medieval songs and themes*). *Art exhibitions, cultural events and musical concerts, together with an important Antiques Fair, complete the broad spectrum of tourist attractions. In the typical small streets of the town centre, one can buy handmade products made by local craftsmen.*

Assisi, a view of the Basilica of St Francis, overlooking the wide green lawn of the piazza Superiore di S. Francesco

THE BASILICA OF ST FRANCIS - The majestic Basilica and Sacred Convent have characterized the serene rural landscape of the Umbrian countryside since remote times. One approaches the building from the *Piazza Inferiore di S. Francesco* (Lower Piazza), an enchanting open space lined with a series of low 15C-16C arcades. The immense structure of the Basilica, regarded as being one of the most famous places of Christian worship, consists of two churches placed one on top of the other: the Lower Church (1228-1230) and the Upper Church (1230-1253). The building is dominated by a robust square **bell tower** in four orders and decorated with mullioned windows of two and three lights and also has large arches. The building was completed in 1239. The Basilica is commonly thought to have been conceived by Friar Elias, the Vicar General of the Franciscans, immediately after the death of St Francis.

The Lower Church: One usually enters the church by means of the fine double portal surmounted by three beautiful rose windows and a portico, added in the 15C. The austere Romanesque-Gothic plan of the building has the form of a double T-shape. The **interior**, which consists of a

Assisi, nocturnal view of the Basilica of St Francis, dominated by the robust square bell tower and the entrance to the Lower Church

single nave divided up into five bays, has a double transept and a semi-circular apse. In the dim light which pervades the whole church, the star-spangled blue vaults are quite breathtaking. To the left of the first bay is the **Chapel of St Sebastian**, decorated with 17C frescoes by G.Martelli and C. Sermei; on the right are two Gothic tombs and a tribune. Through the **Chapel of St Anthony the Abbot** one comes to a small cloister, once the site of a cemetery. Opening out on the right is the **Chapel of St Catherine** with frescoes painted by Andrea da Bologna depicting *Episodes from the Life of St Francis*. Remarkable 13C frescoes by the Maestro di S.Francesco decorate the walls of the nave: on the right are frescoes depicting the *Life of Christ*, whilst on the left are those depicting the *Life of St Francis*. Of note, almost at the end of the left wall, is a Cosmatesque (i.e. of the Cosmati sculptors) tribune with pulpit, embellished with a fresco of the *Coronation of the Virgin* by Puccio Capanna (14C). In the middle part of the nave, a staircase leads down to the **Crypt**, where the sacred remains of St Francis are contained in a stone urn. The **Side Chapels** are all beautifully decorated with 13C-14C stained

Assisi, the interior of the Upper Church, the walls of which are decorated with frescoes by Giotto

glass windows. On the right is the **Chapel of St Stephen** with 16C frescoes by Dono Doni; next to this are the **Chapel of St Anthony of Padua**, decorated by Sermei, and the **Chapel of St Mary Magdalene** with frescoes by Giotto and his school. In the **Chapel of St Martin** (the first on the left) there are some magnificent frescoes painted by Simone Martini depicting the *Saints* and the *Life of St Martin*. In the presbytery, which contains the high Cosmatesque altar (13C), the vaults have frescoes attributed to an unknown pupil of Giotto (known as the Master of the Vaults), which depict the *Allegory of Poverty, Chastity and Obedience* and the *Triumph of St Francis*. In particular, in the right transept one can see frescoes by Giotto and pupils (*Life of Christ and St Francis*), but pride of place goes to the magnificent *Madonna, Child and Angels with St Francis*, one of the most beautiful works by Cimabue, and the *Five Saints* generally believed to be the work of Simone Martini. The **Chapel of St Nicholas** contains frescoes by Giotto and a Gothic tomb of Giovanni Orsini, the work of the Cosmatesque sculptors. The left transept contains not only frescoed ceilings painted by Pietro Lorenzetti and pupils (the *Passion of Christ*), but also some of the Master's most famous works (*Madonna dei Tramonti* ("of the Sunset"), *Crucifixion, The Last Supper, Descent from the Cross, Resurrection of Christ, Entombment*). Another fresco by Lorenzetti (*The Virgin and Child with St Francis and St John*) can also be seen in the **Chapel of St John the Baptist**.

The Upper Church: One enters the church by means of a flight of steps rising from a terrace on the 15C **Large Cloister**, which has two series of arcades. The **interior** is bright and airy, consisting of one nave with a transept and a polygonal apse. A gallery runs along the whole perimeter of the building, which has a well-defined Gothic lay-out and is decorated with cross vaults. 13C frescoes by Cimabue and pupils decorate the walls of the apse and the transept. Although the frescoes have not been well preserved, it is possible to make out the *Story of St Peter*, the *Apocalypse*, the *Crucifixion* and the *Scenes from the Life of the Virgin*. The extraordinary inlaid wooden choir is the work of Domenico Indivini (1491-1501). The frescoes of the *Evangelists* on the vaults above the high altar are also by Cimabue. The upper part of the walls of the nave, embellished by 13C stained glass windows, has a cycle of frescoes (unfortunately badly deteriorated) depicting *Scenes from the Old and New Testaments* (on the right and on the left respectively). These date from

Assisi, frescoes by Giotto in the Upper Church:
a citizen of Assisi pays homage to
St Francis and St Francis receiving
the stigmata on Mt Verna

the second half of the 13C and were painted by Jacopo Torriti and Cimabue's pupils, the most eminent being the young Giotto.

Under the gallery, the walls are covered by a magnificent cycle of twenty-eight frescoes painted by Giotto (however, the last five were completed by his pupils). These depict *Scenes from the Life of St Francis* and show the painter's unique skill and mastery of composition. They are considered to be amongst the finest masterpieces painted by the artist from Mugello.

Among the most interesting features of the **Sacred Convent**, mention should be made of the *Treasury* Museum, which contains valuable, rare illustrated manuscripts, paintings, reliquaries, church ornaments and vestments, altar-frontals and tapestries. It also contains the *Perkins Collection* (14C-15C paintings of the Florentine-Siennese schools). The **façade** of the Upper Church, which faces the town of Assisi and looks out over the wide lawn of the *Piazza Superiore di S. Francesco*, has pure Gothic linear features and is decorated by a large rose window, the work of the Cosmatesque sculptors. This is surrounded by stone reliefs of the *Evangelists*. In the façade is a beautiful double portal.

Assisi. The right transept of the Lower Church, Madonna, Child and Angels with St. Francis, by Cimabue: detail, showing the figure of St Francis

Assisi, Calendimaggio celebrations held in front of the Temple of Minerva in the piazza del Comune

VIA SAN FRANCESCO - One of the most enchanting streets of the ancient town centre, which is in keeping with the characteristic medieval lay-out of the town itself. Here one comes across interesting buildings such as the **Loggia of the Comacini Masters** (13C), in which the builders of Como lived while working on the Basilica of St Francis; the **Pilgrims' Oratory**, once a 15C hospice and subsequently transformed into a chapel, contains frescoes by Matteo da Gualdo and Antonio Mezzastris. The **Portico of Mount Frumentario**, a 13C hospital, and the 16C **Oliviera Fountain** can also be seen along this street.

PIAZZA DEL COMUNE - Situated at the heart of the town and built on the site of the ancient Roman forum, the piazza is surrounded by ancient medieval buildings, and a fountain stands in the middle of the square. Buildings in the piazza include the **Priors' Palace** (14C), which nowadays houses the town council offices, and the **Municipal Picture Gallery** (containing frescoes by the Byzantine, Umbrian and Siennese schools, as well as those painted by the followers of Giotto, paintings by O. Nelli, N. Alunno and Tiberio d'Assisi). To the side of the **Palazzo del Capitano del Popolo** (lit. the Captain of the People's Palace), a turreted 13C building, stands the beautiful **Municipal Tower** (14C), in which the *Bell of Lauds* was placed (1926). Another building in the square is the **Temple of Minerva** which was re-converted into the **Church of St Mary above Minerva** (first half of the 16C, with Baroque transformations added at a later date). This construction is a superb example of a temple of the Augustan period (1C BC.). Worthy of note is the beautiful pronaos, formed by six fluted columns, which rise up from between a flight of steps, with Corinthian capitals supporting a triangular tympanum.

CIVIC MUSEUM - The museum is laid out in the crypt of the **Church of St Nicholas**. Here one can see Etruscan-Roman objects (urns, memorial tablets, gravestones, architectural fragments, remains of sculptures and sarcophagi). A corridor leads from the museum to the ruins of the **Roman Forum** (the original flooring can still be seen), the foundations of the Temple of Minerva, the raised platform of the tribunal and the foundations of an aedicule with statues of *Castor* and *Pollux*.

CHIESA NUOVA (THE NEW CHURCH) - The construction of the church was financed by Philip II of Spain in 1615, and built on property which, according to legend, belonged to St Francis's father, Pietro di Bernardone. Nearby is the **Oratory of the Little Baby Francis**, built above the small stable in which Pica gave birth on the hay strewn floor to the saint of Assisi.

35

Assisi, Cathedral of S. Rufino with its square bell tower and a view of the Basilica of St Clare with its slender bell tower crowned with a spire

THE CATHEDRAL OF S. RUFINO - The building looks out over a piazza bearing the same name, upon which also stands a medieval palace believed to be the house of St Clare's father. The beautiful Romanesque **façade** is divided into three orders. The uppermost order is triangular in shape and has a pointed Gothic arch. The middle order of the façade, divided vertically by pilasters and crowned with a series of small blind arches, is decorated with three magnificent rose windows and stone carvings. At the bottom, there is a tiny gallery which separates the central section of the façade from the lower one, which has three portals. To the side of the Cathedral stands a massive stone **Bell Tower**, adorned with mullioned windows with two lights and blind arches. The **interior**, renovated in the second half of the 16C, according to plans drawn up by Galeazzo Alessi, is divided into a nave and two aisles. The christening font in the right aisle was transferred here from the Cathedral of St Mary of the Bishopric. St Francis, St Clare, St Agnes, St Gabriel "dell'Addolorata" (lit. of our Lady) and the future emperor Frederick II of Swabia were all baptized here. To the left of the high altar is the small **Chapel of the Madonna del Pianto** (lit. the weeping Madonna). In the apse is an outstanding 16C wooden choir. In the **Crypt**, situated underneath the Cathedral, and once part of a pre-existing church, is a *Roman sarcophagus*, which once contained the remains of S. Rufino. Near the left aisle is the entrance to a **Roman Cistern**. From the church one can go through to the **Museo Capitolare (Chapter House Museum)**, which contains the works of Alunno, Matteo da Gualdo and Puccio Capanna.

Assisi, Basilica of St Clare: the Crucifix which, according to legend, spoke to St Francis in the Church of St Damian, and the painting depicting the Life of St Clare, attributed (amongst others) to Cimabue

BASILICA OF ST CLARE - An outstanding example of Gothic-Italian architecture, built in the second half of the 13C and perhaps designed by Filippo da Campello, the Basilica is attached to the Church of St George, in which the body of St Francis was buried before being transferred to its present location. The construction is characterized by three large flying buttresses, which are attached to the left side of the building, while a slender **Bell tower** with a spire rises up from the apse. The beautiful **façade** in three orders, decorated by two coloured horizontal bands of stonework, has a beautiful rose window and a portal. The **interior**, in the form of a Latin cross with one central nave, is simple and bare. A flight of steps leads down to the **Crypt** where the mortal remains of St Clare are contained in a glass coffin. The vault of the presbytery has frescoes by an unknown pupil of Giotto. In the apse, is a beautiful painted *cross*, which was obviously influenced by the paintings of Giunta Pisano. In the left transept is a fresco of the *Nativity* (14C) of Umbrian-Siennese origin. In the right transept is a painting depicting *St Clare* and *Scenes from the Life of St Clare*, believed to be by Cimabue. On the right side of the nave is the entrance to the restored **Church of St George**, in which stands the **Chapel of the Sacrament**, decorated with frescoes in the style of Giotto, and the **Chapel of the Crucifix**, which contains the famous Byzantine painting of a *Crucifix* (12C), which, according to legend, is supposed to have spoken to St Francis in the Church of St Damian. Beyond a lattice window are relics of St Clare and St Francis. At the side of the Basilica stands the imposing **Monastery of the Poor Clares**.

THE CURCH OF S.MARIA MAGGIORE - The building, which is undergoing extensive renovation work in order to restore it to its former splendour, has very ancient origins and was the first Cathedral of Assisi. The present-day Romanesque construction was built in the 12C and designed by Giovanni da Gubbio. It has a simple **façade**, decorated by a beautiful rose window. Near the apse stands the 14C **Bell Tower**. The **interior**, divided into a nave and two aisles, contains the remains of 14C-15C frescoes. Underneath the **Crypt**, the ruins of an ancient Roman building have been unearthed. Next to the church stands the **Bishop's Palace**, where the young Francis renounced his father's wealth in the presence of Bishop Guido.

THE CHURCH OF ST PETER - The church, built in the 13C on the site of a previous church, has elegant Romanesque-Gothic features. The rectangular **façade** in two orders is particularly beautiful. The upper order, completed in 1268, has three magnificent rose windows. The lower section of the façade, decorated at the top by a series of blind arches, has a 12C portal. Worthy of note is the unusual cupola, built on a raised presbytery and a beautiful **Bell Tower** which rises up close to the apse. The **interior**, which has a nave and two aisles, contains 14C frescoes and the ruins of some tombs dating from the same period.

Assisi, the elegant two orders of the façade of the Church of St Peter

Assisi, the Rocca Maggiore dominating the city below

THE GATE OF ST FRANCIS - The main entrance to the town is situated under a turreted tower and set within the town walls, which are quite well-preserved. They extend for a length of almost 5kms and completely surround the medieval part of the town. The other town gates in the walls of Assisi are also situated near defence towers: **St James's Gate, the Perlici Gate, the Cappuccini Gate, the New Gate, the Moiano Gate, the Sementone Gate** and **the Gate of St Peter**.

THE ROCCA MAGGIORE - Passing through the **Perlici Gate** (near which can still be seen the elliptical-shaped area, which was once the site of the **Roman amphitheatre**), one comes to the fortress, which, with its imposing ramparts and towers, dominates the town below. The ancient fortress of Assisi, built before the Lombard occupation, was the scene of many historical events. Once inhabited by Federico Barbarossa in 1174, it was then the home of Corrado di Lutzen, who raised the young Frederick II of Swabia here, until the building was razed to the ground by the inhabitants of Assisi (1198). Rebuilt by the Papal legate, Egidio Albornoz (second half of the 14C), it was later enlarged by Popes Pio II and Paul III. In ancient times, it was attached to the **Rocca Minore (Small Fortress)**, which was reconstructed by the Visconti family.

The Sanctuary of St Damian, just outside Assisi

ENVIRONS

Surrounded by cypress trees and situated just outside the town, is the **Sanctuary of St Damian**. According to legend, the small church, which has a portico, was restored by St Francis (1207) in abeyance to orders given to him by the Crucifix ("Go forth Francis, and rebuild my crumbling house"). Five years later, he brought St Clare and her first followers here. In this spot, which embodies the true Franciscan ideal, Francis wrote his famous *Canticles of All Things Created*. In particular, one can see the **Chapel of St Jerome** (frescoes by Tiberio d'Assisi); the **interior** of the small church (14C frescoes and a 17C wooden *cross* by Fra' Innocenzo da Palermo). Also worth seeing are the **Small Garden** and the **Oratory of St Clare** (the saint died in the small dormitory here).

L'Eremo delle Carceri (lit. **Hermitage of the Cells**) is charmingly located in a densely wooded spot, on Mt Subasio. The serene tranquillity of its location, and the sense of peace and meditation, which pervades the whole environment, make it one of the most peaceful locations along the Franciscan trail. The **Convent** was built near the cave where the saint used to spend many hours praying and meditating. In the 15C, it was enlarged and a church was added. Nearby, the numerous **caves** of the hermits can still be seen.

BASILICA OF ST MARY OF THE ANGELS -The basilica is situated on the plain below Assisi, in a small modern town which bears the same name. The magnificent, immense building was begun in 1569 and designed by Galeazzo Alessi. After being completed in 1679, it was almost immediately rebuilt after being considerably damaged by an earthquake (1832). One can observe the elegant architectural features of the dome, built by Alessi, and the huge golden statue of the Virgin which dominates the church from the top of the **façade**. The solemn, majestic **interior** has a nave and two aisles and contains many Baroque chapels. There are paintings by Il Pomarancio, Appiani, Sermei and other artists. The major attraction of the interior is without doubt the **Porziuncola** (Little Portion, or Portion of Stone), a charming Franciscan oratory, in which the first religious community formed at the "Tugurio" (the hovel) of Rivotorto gathered. In this spot, Clare (of the Scifi family) decided to take her vows of poverty and follow in the footsteps of Francis (1211). The small chapel, situated directly below the imposing dome, is surmounted by a Gothic aedicule and has 14C-15C frescoes. The 19C frescoes on the façade of the chapel are by F. Overbeck. In the deeply mystical atmosphere of the **interior** is a large painted panel (polyptych) on the high altar by Ilario da Viterbo (14C). St Francis died in the nearby **Cappella del Transito (Chapel of the Passing Away of the Saint)** (3-10-1226); here there are frescoes by Spagna (16C) and an enamelled terracotta statue of *St Francis* by Andrea della Robbia. An altar-frontal in the **Crypt** is also the work of the artist. Other features of the Basilica include the **Chapel of the Rose** with frescoes by Tiberio d'Assisi, the **Miraculous Rose Garden** and the **Convent** (in which the **Ethnographical Museum of Missionary Work** is located, as well as a collection of art works, including works by Maestro di S. Francesco, Giunta Pisano and others).

A view of the Hermitage of the Cells, situated along the green slopes of Mt Subasio (Assisi)

ATTIGLIANO

A small town with ancient origins, situated at the end of a terracing facing the Val Tiberina (the Upper Tiber), between the Florence-Rome railway track and the "Sole" motorway. There is reason to believe that the origins of the place date back to Roman times, even if the territory was almost certainly a settlement during the Etruscan period, as the archaeological finds of Marziano and Jana have testified (these include chamber tombs and crypts, which are definitely of Etruscan origin).

Amongst the most popular folk events are the festival of the patron saint, *St Laurence* (10 August) and the *Christmas Concert* with the "*Nativity Play*" (a re-enactment of the Christmas story), which are put on to great effect in the ancient town centre.

Worthy of note is the **Castle**, or rather what remains of the ancient fortress, which has five turreted towers and a pentagonal look-out tower. Founded by the successors of Count Offredo, it was then reconstructed during the time of Bartolomeo d'Alviano, when a large cannon was added. Alongside the tower in the 16C, stood the *Baronial Palace*, which was later enlarged by the Farnese, before being demolished in relatively recent times.

The *Piazza of the Fortress* is, without doubt, one of the most interesting features of the town and reminds one of bygone splendour, as opposed to the present-day neglect and desolation. Here stands the ancient **Parish Church** (16C) which has a plain portal and adjoining bell tower, and a **Bell tower** which has a 12 hour clock with only one hand.

AVIGLIANO UMBRO

The commune, which includes the villages of Dunarobba, Santa Restituta, Sismano and Toscolano, was formed in 1975 and is therefore, in administrative terms, of fairly recent origins. The various villages are dotted along the hills situated between the Valle Umbra and the Val Tiberina. The territories of Avigliano were densely populated during Roman times, thanks to the fact that the *Via Flaminia* and *Via Ulpiana* facilitated links between this region and the capital. Apart from a round **Turreted Tower** and ruins of the **town walls** with a **Gate** bearing the coat of arms of Todi (*an Eagle protecting two eaglets*), very few traces of its medieval past can be seen in the modern town. In the countryside of Avigliano, there is a sturdy **Clock Tower** crowned with merlons.

In the village of **Dunarobba** stands a **Fortress**. In spite of the fact that it is nowadays used as an agricultural store-house, the features of a medieval stone manor-house with robust, round corner towers are still visible. In the same spot is the **Fossil Forest**, made up of enormous upright tree-trunks which date back to the Early Pleistocene era.

Worth seeing at **Sismano** is the **castle**, which has lateral towers and dominates the 14C houses of the medieval village below.

Finally, mention should be made of the recently explored **Beautiful Grotto**, in the district of Avigliano, which is characterized by its wealth of mineral concretions. Archaeological work inside the grotto has uncovered findings which date back to the Apennine settlements of the Bronze Age.

BASCHI

Picturesque Umbrian town with prominent medieval features, Baschi stands on a ridge dominating the Valtiberina, a short way downstream from the confluence of the Paglia river. Below the town, lies a stretch of the A1 motorway (the Orvieto to Attigliano section). The origins of the town date back to Roman times, but Baschi enjoyed its period of greatest splendour in the Middle Ages. During this period, the noble family of Baschi, who were the owners of the town and its surrounding district, built a castle on this spot, which soon became part of the possessions of Orvieto. After the setting up of a free commune (15C), Baschi became established as one of the territories controlled by the Church.

The typical features of medieval building work can still be seen in the village today, even if nothing remains of the impressive defence systems of long ago. The only outstanding element is the **Church of St Nicholas**,

Baschi, a picturesque view of the medieval village near Lake Corbara

built in the second half of the 16C, and designed by Ippolito Scalza. In the interior is a 15C polyptych of the Siennese school (Giovanni di Paolo). The small village of **Civitella del Lago**, forms part of the commune. It was built on the site where the Roman settlement of *Civitula* once stood, in an area populated since ancient times. During medieval times, a castle was built here which allowed its owners to control the underlying valley of the Tiber. Today, the large artificial lake of **Corbara** can be seen in the valley, which stretches out like a Nordic fjord in the idyllic landscape of the Umbrian hills.

BASTIA UMBRA

An important centre in the Valle Umbra, it lies in the plain lapped by the waters of the Chiascio river, downstream from the confluence of the Tescio river. Although the origins of Bastia Umbra would seem to date back to Roman times, the first definite references to the place date from the second half of the 11C, when it was known as *Insula Romana*. From the beginning of the 13C it was controlled by Assisi, and in the 14C it became known as *Bastia* due to the numerous defence structures built during a period of continual strife between the cities of Perugia and Assisi. Today Bastia Umbra is a thriving agricultural, industrial and commercial centre, and traditional fairs and festivals have been held here since an-

Bastia Umbra, an important town situated along the Chiascio plain: nocturnal view of the Church of S. Croce

cient times (Regional Centre "Umbriafiera Maschiella"). Amongst the most genuine expressions of local folklore, mention should be made of the *Procession of the Rinchinata* (lit. Procession of Kneeling), which is held at Easter, and the *Palio of St Michael the Archangel* (competition between the town districts held on the Patron Saint's Feast Day).

The **Gate of S.Angelo** is the best preserved of the five gates, which once stood within the ancient external town walls. Very little remains of the ancient fortifications: the castle and the seventeen bastions, which reinforce the town walls. The **Church of St Paul** is situated near the cemetery; it is a Romanesque construction, which was once part of the monastery bearing the same name. References to the building date back to the end of the 12C. The **Church of S. Croce** has a 14C façade. The interior, in the Gothic style, has detached frescoes painted by Tiberio d'Assisi and B. Caporali. There is also an admirable triptych by N. Alunno (end of the 15C). At the centre of the ancient manor-house stands the **Church of S. Angelo**; it has extremely ancient origins, even if the present building is the result of 15C reconstruction work. Finally, note should also be made of the modern **Parish Church of St.Michael the Archangel** and the **Votive Church of S. Rocco** (first half of the 17C), which has a standard by Dono Doni in its interior.

BETTONA

Once known as *Vettona* and still, for the most part, contained within the ancient town walls, Bettona lies on the summit of a green hill covered with olive groves, situated along the first northern spurs of the Martani Mountains. The first inhabitants of the place were most probably Etruscans - a hypothesis backed up by the numerous archaeological finds discovered here. In Roman times, Bettona was first a colony, before later becoming a town. Today Bettona is mainly a rural centre and well-known for its considerable production of furniture. Local folklore events include the *Procession of the Dead Christ* (Good Friday) and the *Festival of S.Crispolto* (May). For the most part, the **town walls** of Bettona date back to the medieval period. A large part of the walls of Bettona were built during Etruscan times and date back to the 4C BC. The **Church of St Mary** dates from the 13C. In the interior are works by Perugino, N. Alunno and an *Assumption* of the Siennese school. Amongst the other places of worship, mention should be made of the 13C **Abbey of S.Crispolto**, the **Oratory of St Andrew** and the **Convent of S. Onofrio**, decorated with 14C frescoes. The beautiful **Palace of the Podestà** dates from the 15C and houses the interesting *Municipal Picture Gallery*. The gallery includes works by Andrea della Robbia, Tiberio d'Assisi, Dosso

Bettona, the fountain in Piazza Garibaldi and the bell tower of the Church of St Mary situated nearby

Bevagna, decorative features of the Romanesque Church of St Sylvester

Dossi, Fiorenzo di Lorenzo and Pietro Vannucci (Perugino). There are also Etruscan-Roman exhibits on show. Mention should also be made of the plaster-finished **Baglioni Palace**, which, in fact, has ancient origins and was the home of the Baglioni Counts of Bettona. A little outside the town, on the road to **Colle**, there is an Etruscan **Tomb** dating from the 2C BC. Worthy of note in the small village of **Passaggio** are the **Abbey of S. Crispolto** and the **Villa of the Boccaglione Family**, - an 18C building believed to be the work of Piermarini.

BEVAGNA

An important town in the Foligno district, Bevagna is situated near the foothills of the Martani Mountains. There is documentary evidence to suggest that the surrounding areas were inhabited since the Iron Age. Even up to the present day, Bevagna has managed to retain its overall medieval character, although the Roman configuration of the town is

Bevagna, the splendid façade of the Romanesque Cathedral of St Michael the Archangel

still largely evident. The *Piazza Filippo Silvestri* is counted as being one of the most beautiful of the region and is characterized by its pleasant medieval ambience. The **Church of St Domenic and St James** (13C) stands on the site of a pre-existing oratory. The **Consuls' Palace** is a beautiful example of 13C architecture, with an external flight of steps, a double order of mullioned windows with two lights and a Gothic portico on the ground floor. The **Church of St Sylvester** is a beautiful Romanesque building completed by the Cosmatesque sculptor, Binello, in 1195, as testified by the plaque on the side of a fine portal decorated by *Christian symbols*. The enchanting façade which is built in travertine and pink Subasio stone is decorated by a mullioned window with three lights and by two lateral mullioned windows with two lights with small twisted columns. At the top of the façade is a relief decorated with animal sculptures. The arrangement of the buildings lining the piazza, which is decorated with a beautiful polygonal fountain, is further enhanced by the **Cathedral of St Michael the Archangel**. This graceful Romanesque construction was built in the 12C, based upon a plan by the Cosmatesque sculptors Binello and Rodolfo, but was subjected to many reconstructions between the 18C-19C . The splendid façade has three portals; the middle portal is rich in decorative motifs. The upper portion of the façade is decorated by two mullioned windows with three lights on each side, above which stands a string-course of blind arches.

The **Town Hall** was reconstructed in the 18C and houses the *Archives,* the *Library* and the *Municipal Picture Gallery.* The gallery contains works by Dono Doni, Fantino di Bevagna (A.Spacca), Camassei, Filippo Angeli and works by the Venetian school. In *Piazza Garibaldi* stand the few remaining ruins of a **Roman Temple**. The ruins of the building, believed to date back to the 2C AD., are only barely visible. In a building along the *Via Guelfa* it is possible to see a remarkable **Roman Mosaic** (first half of the 2C AD.). The mosaic, which was examined and studied by experts during the 17C, is made up of small black and white tesserae and depicts a *Horse ridden by a Triton, Two Dolphins, a Lobster, Two Polyps*. Close by, one can see the remains of the supporting structures of the tiers and the cavea of the **Roman Theatre**.

CALVI DELL'UMBRIA

The village is situated on a woody hill, dominated by Mount St Pancras and by other mountains over 1000m in height. Dominating the Valtiberina, it has become a well-known holiday resort. Probably built in Roman times, it then became a possession of the Abbots of Farfa, and then fell into the hands of the Orsini and Anguillara families.

Amongst the traditional folk events held here, mention should be made of the *Nativity Play* (a re-enactment of the Christmas Story) (December-January) and the *Palio of the Donkeys* (August). Among the most important artistic features of Calvi is a **Holy Crib**, dating from 1546, which has large terracotta statues, situated in the *Church of St Anthony*. This church shares its façade (designed by Fuga) with the **Church of St Paul**. A little outside the town stands the **Church of St Francis**.

CANNARA

The village is situated at the centre of the Valle Umbra, near the confluence of the Timia-Teverone and the Topino rivers. The historical origins of the place are believed by some to date back to the hill-top Roman settlement of *Urvinum Hortense* (the present-day Collemancio, situated on the northernmost reaches of the Martani Mountains). The historical centre of modern-day Cannara is well defined and lies to the left of the Topino river, while on the opposite part of the river, towns of more recent origins have sprung up. Amongst the local folk events, mention should be made of the *Procession of the Dead Christ* (Good Friday), the *Rinchinata* (Easter), the *Infiorate* (Corpus Domini), and the *Re-enactment of the Christmas Story* (Christmas). Amongst the salient features of the village, mention should be made of the **Church of the Buona Morte**; the 18C **Church of St Matthew**; the **Church of St Blaze**; the **Church of St John the Baptist**. On the road to Bevagna, at **Pian d'Arca**, an aedicule commemorates the spot where St Francis preached to the birds. Worth seeing in the small town of **Collemancio** are the 15C **Palace of the Podestà**, and above all the **archaeological site**.

Cascia, a panoramic view of the small town surrounded by the typical Umbrian countryside

CASCIA

HISTORICAL BACKGROUND - *Well-known tourist resort in the district of Valnerina, the town of Cascia is huddled around the Colle S. Agostino, lapped by the winding course of the river Corno, and surrounded by a chain of green mountains. The town, together with Assisi, is a religious centre of world-wide fame, associated with the memory of St Rita, who was born here and lived in Cascia up until the time of her death. An ancient Reatine foundation (6C-5C BC.), it subsequently fell into the hands of the Umbrians, the Etruscans, the Sabines and the Romans, who built the centre of* Cursula *here. Destroyed by an earthquake (63 BC.) and rebuilt, it was then razed to the ground by the Goths (4C), plundered by the Lombards (6C) and destroyed once again by the Saracens (9C). Having become an autonomous Republic in the 12C, it underwent a period of change and up-heaval during the struggles with the neighbouring city and the disputes be-tween the Guelphs and the Ghibelline factions. In the second half of the 15C, Pope Paul II ordered a fortress to be built on top of the hill, in order to take military control of the town. In the first half of the 16C, Cascia was sub-jected to the attempts on behalf of the followers of the Roman family of Colonna to take control of the fortress. The sacking of the town by the armies of Sciarra Colonna (1527) and a further conflict with Spoleto con-tributed even further to the downfall of the town, which also suffered seri-ous damage during several earthquakes (1599, 1703, 1950, 1962). More re-cently, the catastrophic earthquake of 19 September 1979 inflicted a harsh blow on the art and the monuments of the Valnerina. A clear example of its devastating effects is to be seen at the 16C Sanctuary of the Madonna of the Snow (built by Bramante, containing frescoes by the Camillo brothers and by Fabio Angelucci), which was almost totally destroyed in the earthquake. Amongst the most typical products of the local handicraft industry are tex-tiles, wrought-iron work, wooden objects and copperware, as well as wick-er work and terracotta objects. As in many other Umbrian centres, local folk events are closely bound to religious celebrations; these include the* Procession of the Dead Christ *(Good Friday) and the* Fire of the Faith *(a charming "Luminaria", in which the whole town is lit up by thousands of small torches on the eve of St Rita's Day) (21 May).*

45

BASILICA OF ST RITA -The modern basilica has become a characteristic feature of the landscape around Cascia. Work on its construction was begun in 1936, when it was decided to replace the pre-existing small church with a larger building, in order to accommodate the ever-increasing number of pilgrims who came to pay homage to the remains of St Rita. The design of Monsignor Spirito Chiapetta, re-elaborated by Martinenghi and Calori, was completed in 1940. Having been opened as a place of worship eight years later, the building was then consecrated as a basilica by a Papal decree signed by Pio XII (1955). The building, which was influenced by features of Romanesque-Byzantine architecture, has a white travertine **façade**, which has two twin bell towers on either side. At the side of the portal are some reliefs executed by E.Pellini, depicting *Scenes from the Life of St Rita*; above the architrave is a large *Cross*, sustained by statues of angels. The **interior** is in the shape of a Greek cross and contains many modern works of art. A women's gallery runs along the whole perimeter of the building. The high altar, by Giacomo Manzù, was placed here in 1981, during the celebrations held to commemorate the 600th anniversary of the birth of St Rita (1381-1447). Amongst the numerous contemporary frescoes, which adorn the walls of the church are : *The Paradise of the Augustinian Saints* (**Cupola**, L.Montanarini); *Exhaltation of the Cross* (**Apse at the entrance**, S.Consadori); *Glorification of St Rita* (**Chapel of St Rita**, F.Ferrazzi); *Assumption* (**Chapel of Our Lady of the Assumption**, G.Ceracchini); *Last Supper* (**Chapel of the Sacrament**, L.Filocamo). All of these frescoes were painted between 1950 and 1956. The stations of the *Cross*, executed in marble, are by E.Pellini. The **Chapel of St Rita** is the most interesting feature of the interior in both artistic and religious terms. Its architectural style is a modern re-working of Byzantine motifs and models. The urn containing the body of the saint stands on a marble plinth, which has decorations along its front by Pellini. On the exterior corners of the urn are sculptures of the *Cardinal Virtues*, in gilded bronze. The vaulted ceiling of the chapel has eight frescoed medallions depicting the *Augustinian Saints* by F.Taragni. Some works by G.B.Galizi, along the walls, depict *Scenes from the Life of St Rita*. The so-called **Lower Basilica** is a modern building, constructed at the end of the 1980s, as a result of restructuring work carried out on the pre-existing crypt. A silver ostensory contains the venerated "Sacred Relic" of Corpus Christi, and the tomb of Mother Maria Teresa Fasce, patron of the construction of the new sanctuary can also be seen. The "Sacred Relic" was brought to Cascia by Beato Simone Fidati in 1335. In the Archives of Cascia is a detailed description of the miracle written in archaic Italian by an anonymous historian from the convent of St Augustine in Perugia. The holy relic, worshipped by numerous pilgrims and popes, has, over the centuries, been stored in several different reliquaries. Nowadays during religious festivals the "Sacred Relic" is displayed in an extremely valuable gold ostensory which has intricate carvings.

PENITENTIARY - This unusual building which consists of a series of four inter-connecting rooms, was inaugurated on the 10th of May 1986. The project, which was designed and built under the supervision of the architects Caproni, Gengo and Scrimieri was originally conceived during the festivities held to commemorate the conversion of St Augustine. One enters the penitentiary by turning left outside the Basilica of St Rita and descending a flight of steps. At the bottom of these steps is an allegorical sculpture by Armando Marrocco depicting *The Fountain of Life*. The doors of the entrance are decorated with scenes depicting the *Four Cardinal Virtues* by Marrocco. This artist's works can be admired throughout the complex: the Reception Hall contains a sculpture depicting the *Prodigal Son*; a bronze *Crucifix* can be seen in the Room where worshippers prepare for confession; finally, *Christ Resurrected* (considered to be Armando Marrocco's masterpiece) can be seen in the Thanksgiving Room. This visually striking work betrays great interpretative vigour and is one of this contemporary artist's best works which can be admired in the city of St Rita.

THE MONASTERY OF ST RITA - The building stands near the basilica and belonged originally to the Benedictines, becoming an Augustinian monastery in the first half of the 14C. Amongst the features of the monastery worth visiting are the 16C **Cloister**, with a gallery running along a part of the upper order, containing the so-called "miraculous vine"; the **Oratory**, where St Rita received the stigmata (1432), and the **Cell** where the saint lived and died. Here one can see the *Sarcophagus* (painted by an unknown artist) in which St Rita's body was placed after her death in 1457.

TOWN HALL - This building looks out over *Piazza Aldo Moro.* Its simple, elegant features are the result of several transformations carried out over the centuries. Originally, it was a noble residence belonging to the Frenfanelli family who moved here from Foligno after the earthquake of 1703 caused considerable damage to the city. Of the original building, only the two portals and archivolts decorated with characteristic ashlar stone, remain. To the side of the building, at the end of a small lane, stands a travertine bell tower, built in the first half of the 18C. The bell itself was made in the 14C and weighs around 20 quintals (2000 kilograms).

CHURCH OF ST FRANCIS - This Gothic building was constructed in the first half of the 15C, and the eastern side contains some remaining architectural features of a 13C church and annexed monastery which were dismantled in modern times. The **façade**, in two orders, is separated by a string-course and is decorated by an impressive rose window and a beautiful splayed Gothic portal. The lunette is decorated with a 15C fresco (*Madonna and Child with St Francis and St Clare*). The **interior** with a Latin cross plan has 17C stucco decorations. Numerous frescoes include the *Virgin and Child* by Siennese artists of the 15C (on the left); *St Anthony of Padua, St Anthony the Abbot and Catherine of Alexandria*, by the Umbrian school (15C, on the right); *Trinity and Adoration of the Shepherds* (near the 17C wooden pulpit) and *St Benedict*, both by Bartolomeo di Tommaso da Foligno (15C). Another interesting feature is the beautiful 14C wooden choir. Near the altar of St Francis (on the left cross vault), is a powerful interpretation of the *Ascension* (second half of the 16C) by Niccolò Circignani (Il Pomarancio).

PIAZZA GARIBALDI - The square is the main hub of town life and a popular meeting place for its inhabitants. In the past there were two separate squares: piazza S. Spirito and piazza S. Francesco. In 1861 the whole area became known as piazza del Mercato (the Market square) and then later as piazza Garibaldi and piazza Vittorio Emanuele 11, thereby re-establishing the area into two separate squares. In 1971 the entire area was dedicated to the "Hero of the Two Worlds" (Garibaldi).

THE COLLEGIATE CHURCH OF ST MARY - An extremely ancient building, existing as far back as 856, it is believed to have been built in the Early Christian era on pre-existing Roman ruins. Once the seat of the parish priest, it became the seat of the archpriest (or dean) in the first half of the 17C. The numerous transformations to which it has been subjected have left few traces of the original Romanesque construction
The upper portion of the bare and simple **façade** was restored after the earthquake of 1962. One of its ancient stone lions can still be seen (the other is now situated at a nearby fountain). The **interior** of the church has a nave and two aisles. It contains some sections of frescoes by Nicolò da Siena (15C): *Crucifixion, Deposition and Nativity.* Finally, two 16C paintings by Gaspare and Camillo Angelucci da Mevale (*Peace amongst the inhabitants of Cascia*) and by Nicola Frangipane (*Mysteries of the Rosary*) are also to be seen. Other works of art are contained in the sacristy, the most outstanding being a valuable 15C wooden sculpture of *St Sebastian* by followers of Antonio Rizzo.

THE CHURCH OF ST ANTHONY THE ABBOT - The building to be seen today was built between the 14C and the 15C on the site of an ancient 11C church (which subsequently collapsed). The church was damaged by an earthquake at the beginning of the 18C. In the hall-like **interior**, there is an outstanding apse with a cycle of 16 frescoes, depicting *Scenes from the Life of St Anthony the Abbot.* In the semi-calotte of the vault is a painting of the *Four Evangelists.* Some medallions situated in the intrados of the apse depict the *Twelve Apostles.* Finally, mention should be made of an *Annunciation* on the back wall and some paintings of the *Passion of Christ* in the choir of the ex-monastery, completed in the second half of the 15C by Nicola da Siena.

Cascia, the Church of St Augustine and its adjoining convent stand in a scenic position dominating the town below

THE CHURCH OF ST AUGUSTINE - The church and the adjoining convent are situated in a pleasant panoramic position dominating the town below. Considered to be one of the most ancient Augustinian buildings in Umbria, it is thought to have existed as far back as the 11C on the site of an ancient temple, which was transformed into a place of Christian worship. The present church dates from the second half of the 14C. The construction, built entirely of square stone blocks, has a **façade** decorated by a deeply splayed Gothic portal. In the lunette is a 15C fresco of the Umbrian school (*Virgin and Child*).

The **interior** has one nave and contains 15C frescoes. Depicted on the right is a *Virgin* (within an almond-shaped niche) and *on the left, St Augustine and St Rita*; a 17C wooden pulpit; a *Madonna and Child* (16C).

FORTRESS - Near the Church of St Augustine, on a hill bearing the same name, stand numerous ruins of bastions and walls of an ancient fortress built by Battista di Castiglione, in the second half of the 15C. Its construction was ordered by Pope Paul II, in order to control both the restless inhabitants of Cascia and its delicately strategic position, given that the territory lay in a spot which marked the boundary between the Papal possessions and those of the Kingdom of Naples. The fortress only remained standing for a few decades, because Leo X then ordered it to be dismantled (1517), after it had become a meeting point for the adversaries of Church policies.

ENVIRONS

ROCCAPORENA

Pleasantly situated in a wild and inaccessible valley, which is nonetheless shrouded in captivating beauty, stands the village of Roccaporena, one of the most characteristic spots of the Valnerina. The village, dominated by the bizarre, soaring outline of the Rock of St Rita is famous for being the birthplace of Margherita Mancini, who later became St Rita. Amongst the most interesting tourist features are the **House of St Rita** (transformed into a chapel in the first half of the 17C; the painting on the altar depicts the *Saint receiving the stigmata* by Luca Giordano); the **Lazzeretto** (once an ancient hospital, with a portico decorated with frescoes); the **Sanctuary** (a modern construction inaugurated in 1946). The *Statue of St Rita*, in the pronaos, was executed in 1968 by V. Crocetti. In the interior are numerous mosaics depicting *Saints*; the **Parish Church of S.Montano** (13C) was the scene of many important episodes in the life

Cascia: the Rock of St Rita; house of St Rita (which has now been converted into a chapel); the modern façade of the Sanctuary of St Rita

*Cascia, the Church of S. Montano and the Garden of the Miracle
(bronze statue by Maleci)*

of St Rita. The saint is portrayed in many paintings in the interior; the **Garden of St Rita** (here, there is a bronze statue by R. Maleci, depicting the miraculous event of a rose in bloom and figs maturing in the heart of winter, being picked by a relative of the dying saint).

The imposing outline of the **Rock of St Rita** (also known as the *Rock of Prayer*)surrounded by trees and rocks, dominates the idyllic village below. A path which has been widened and lined with the *Stations of the Way of the Cross* leads to the summit (827 m). The *Chapel* on the summit was rebuilt in 1981 after the earthquake of 1979. An earlier chapel, reconstructed in 1941, was built here in 1929. From the summit of the "Rock" there are beautiful views of Roccaporena and the surrounding green hills of Cascia.

In the village of **Ocosce** stands the 14C **Church of St Mary of Loreto**. The fine stone façade has a beautiful pointed Gothic portal. The interior, which has one nave, contains a masterly 15C *Madonna*, an interesting example of polychrome sculpture in the Abruzzo style (Silvestro dell'Aquila).

The **Castle of St Mary** has been entirely rebuilt and is emblematic of the catastrophic earthquake, which struck the Valnerina on the 19th of September, 1979. The devastation brought about by this seismic event was responsible for the almost complete destruction of (amongst others) the outstanding **Sanctuary of the Madonna of the Snow**. Unfortunately, all that remains of this wonderful octagonal-shaped building (probably built in the second half of the 16C, designed by Bramante) is a large number of ruins.

CERRETO DI SPOLETO

Picturesque village dominating the valleys of the Vigi and the Nera rivers, which is surrounded by a ring of high mountains. References to the place date back to 13C documents, and it was later contended between the nearby towns of Spoleto and Norcia.

In the main square of the village stands the **Church of Our Lady of the Assumption**. The building was restored after the earthquake of 1703.

Amongst the civic buildings of Cerreto, mention should be made of the **Town Hall**, the houses of the **Toni**, **Nobili**, and **Vespasiani** noble families and the 15C **Civic Tower**.

The **Church of St Nicholas**, which unfortunately now lies in ruins, dates from the 13C. The **Church of the Ex-Monastery of St James** has 14C-15C frescoes. The **Church of St Mary of Libera** is a unique two-floored 15C-16C construction. In the village of **Borgo Cerreto** stands the lovely **Church of St Laurence**.

CITERNA

Pleasantly situated on a hilly ridge dominating the Valtiberina, Citerna is situated close to the Tuscan border. Founded by the Etruscans, it was inhabited by the Romans who named it *Castrum Citernae*.

The **Town Walls**, some parts of which are very well preserved, contain notable remains of communication trenches, bastions and round turreted towers.

The **Church of St Francis** was built in 1316 and rebuilt in 1508.

The **Church of The Holy Cross** is the result of extension work carried out on an ancient building in the first half of the 16C. The church was restored after damage caused by a cyclone (1890) and an earthquake in 1917. Finally, another interesting feature is the 16C fireplace, to be seen in the **Prosperi-Vitelli House**. In the tiny village of **Pistrino**, one should not forget to visit the **Church of Our Lady of the Assumption**. The construction dates back to the 15C and is worth a visit as it contains interesting Renaissance frescoes of the Umbrian school.

CITTÀ DELLA PIEVE

A charming medieval town pleasantly set out along a hilly ridge, between the river courses of the Chiani and the Nestore, Città della Pieve is situated in the enchanting setting of the Umbrian hills, a short distance from the Tuscan border. Probably built in Etruscan times, as a dependency of Chiusi, it became a municipality under the Romans. After having been conquered by the Lombards, it was then donated to the Church by the Carolingian dynasty. At the turn of the 12C, it was acquired by the Papacy, and the status of a town was conferred upon it by Pope Clement VIII (1601). The town, previously known as *Pieve di S. Gervasio* and *Castel della Pieve*, is universally famous for being the birthplace of the great Renaissance painter, Pietro Vannucci. The artist, who is known by the nickname "Perugino", has handed down to posterity a wealth of paintings depicting the life and colours of the fascinating landscape of hills and lakes around the Trasimeno area.

Nowadays, Città della Pieve has an enchanting aura, conferred upon it by its picturesque arrangement of ancient brick constructions, which seem to keep vigil over the rolling hills dotted by the lakes of Trasimeno, Chiusi and Montepulciano. The lively atmosphere of the medieval town, with its wealth of artistic and historical heritage, the char-

Città della Pieve, an external view of the ancient medieval walls

acteristic ironwork produced by local craftsmen and the historical connotations of the *Palio dei Terzieri* (Cart Race) (second Sunday in August) are all factors which contribute to make Città della Pieve an extremely interesting tourist town.

Piazza Gramsci lies at the heart of the town, and it is here that the **Cathedral of SS. Gervasio and Protasio** is located. The building (12C) was substantially reconstructed during the course of the 16C and the 17C. On the site of the modern building, an ancient Early Christian Church (reconverted from a pagan temple) once stood. To the side of the façade stands the **Public Tower**, a masterly example of Romanesque (travertine sections) and Gothic architecture (brick sections), with mullioned windows with two and four lights. The tower measures 38 metres in height. The interior of the church, which has a Latin cross plan, has one nave and several side chapels. Below the apse are the remains of a 14C crypt. Amongst the numerous works of art, mention should be made of two frescoes by Perugino depicting *The Baptism of Christ* and *Madonna and Child with St Peter, St Paul, S.Gervasio and S.Protasio*; a 16C fresco by Alfani of *The Virgin and Child with St Martin, St Mary Magdalene and Angels*; the fresco in the apse by Il Pomarancio (N.Circignani) of *The Eternal and Angels*; and a wooden *Crucifix* (16C), probably the work of the pupils of Giambologna. Near the Sacristy is a small *Museum* containing interesting paintings, detached frescoes and jewellery belonging to the Diocese.

The **Mazzuoli** *(ex-Della Corgna)* **Palace** was built by Alessi in the second half of the 16C. The vaults of the interior have frescoes with decorative motifs, painted by the Florentine artist Salvio Savini (1580).

The ancient *Oratory of the Disciplined*, today annexed to the **Church of S.Maria della Mercede** (lit. of the reward) (or *dei Bianchi*), was built as an 18C extension to a previous church and is famous for the fact that it contains a large fresco by Perugino, which is considered to be the artist's masterpiece amongst the works on display in his native town: *Epiphany* (1504) or the *Adoration of the Magi*, as it is more commonly known.

The turreted **fortress** was built by the Perugians in the first half of the 14C and was enlarged and reinforced in the following century. It was in this building that Cesare Borgia gave orders for Paolo Orsini and the Duke of Gravina to be strangled to death, so as to gain revenge after a plot had been organized to overthrow him at Magione. The *Castellana*, *Maestra* and *Serpentina* towers still remain today; two other towers were knocked down during the first half of the 17C.

The **Church of St Augustine**, which is nowadays used for cultural events, was constructed towards the middle of the 13C and then later rebuilt. Here, one can admire a beautiful *Ascension* by Il Pomarancio (N.Circignani) and two paintings by Salvio Savini, depicting *The Madonna with Saints and Brothers* and *Scenes from the Life of S.Nicola da Tolentino*. The **Sanctuary of the Madonna di Fatima** (once the *Church of St Francis*) is the result of partial reconstruction work (18C) carried out on the original 13C building. The brick façade has three blind arches; to be seen in the interior are a *Pentecost* by Niccolò Circignani and an *Enthroned Virgin and Saints* by D. Alfani. Nearby stands the **Oratory of St Bartholomew** which contains a 15C *Madonna and Child with St Francis and St Anthony of Padua* and a large fresco by Maestro degli Ordini (influenced by the works of Taddeo Gaddi (1342-1360)) depicting the *Crucifixion*, more commonly known as the *Pianto degli angeli* (*The Weeping of the Angels*).

The **Church of St Peter**, once known as the *Church of St Anthony the Abbot*, is the result of reconstruction work done on a pre-existing church, carried out at the beginning of the 16C. It contains a fresco by Perugino (painted on a canvas) which can only partially be made out, depicting *St Anthony the Abbot enthroned between S.Marcello and St Peter the Hermit*.

Where a place of worship dedicated to the *Madonna of the Star* once stood, the **Church of S.Maria dei Servi** was built during the 13C and 14C. It later underwent Baroque reconstruction work (17C). In the interior, one can admire a masterly *Deposition* by Perugino, which recent restoration work has now restored to its former splendour. Finally, mention should be made of the Baroque **Della Fargna Palace** (18C), the present seat of the Town Council, and the **Bandini Palace** (16C) originally a 14C construction, re-designed by the young Alessi.

Città di Castello, a view over the town and the surrounding countryside of the Valtiberina

CITTÀ DI CASTELLO

HISTORICAL BACKGROUND - *Umbria's northernmost city in the Upper Valtiberina, situated to the left of the Tiber (as seen on the map), lying almost at the heart of the valley, Città di Castello is a lively tourist town, full of important medieval and Renaissance buildings. Originally an Umbrian foundation, it had some dealings with the Etruscans, although it still retained its independence. As a part of the Early Roman Empire at the turn of the IC AD, it became a flourishing municipality known as* Tifernum Tiberinum. *The Roman town was further enlarged by the construction of temples and public buildings, and Pliny the Younger proved to be an excellent patron to the town. Razed to the ground by the armies of Totila, it was then rebuilt by Bishop Florido into a fortress town. It fell firstly into the hands of the Byzantines and then to the Lombards and was referred to as* Castrum Felicitatis *in a document dating from the 8C. Passing from the Franks to the control of the Church, Città di Castello became a free town (12C), when, once again, its name was changed to* Civitas Castelli *(from which the actual place name is derived). Growing in importance and power, it extended its territorial possessions beyond the Apennines, while, with the advent of the Vitelli family (end of the 15C), new churches and palaces soon flourished, whose Tuscan-Renaissance architectural features still characterize the present day city. Valentino (Cesare Borgia) took control of the city for the Papacy and, even though it was later subjected to periods of upheaval, it remained a Papal possession until it was annexed to the Kingdom of Italy (1860).*

THE CATHEDRAL OF SS. FLORIDO AND AMANZIO - The discovery of ancient architectural features has backed up the hypothesis that the present day construction was built on the site where Pliny the Younger had previously constructed a church. The Cathedral, which still contains traces of the restructuring work carried out during the Gothic period, has a magnificent **façade** divided into sections by columns, pilaster strips and niches. The construction has an intriguing round 13C **bell tower** with a spire and bears obvious similarities to the Byzantine style of the towers of Ravenna. The **interior** of the church has a Latin cross plan with one nave and has a decidedly 16C layout, even if numerous features have obviously been borrowed from 15C Florentine architecture. The coffered ceiling dates from the end of the 17C. One of the most outstanding side chapels is that of the **Holy Sacrament** which contains the *Transfiguration of Christ* (first half of the 16C) by Rosso Fiorentino. The **Lower Church** (15C) has an 18C altar and a sarcophagus containing both the relics of the patron saints and other local saints. In the adjoining **Cathedral Museum** one can see the highly valuable *Treasure of the Sanctuary of Canoscio*, a collection which includes numerous examples of Early Christian art (5C-6C).

TOWN HALL - A masterly example of 14C architecture, the building was designed by Angelo da Orvieto. The rough stonework of its façade and the charming trilobal mullioned windows with two lights on the upper order contribute to the overall elegance of the building.

BISHOP'S TOWER - This square, slender, stone construction was built in the 13C. The earthquake of 1789 (in which the small roof above the entrance tower collapsed) greatly damaged a fresco by Luca Signorelli (*The Enthroned Virgin and Child with St Peter and St Paul*) above the entrance door.

PALACE OF THE PODESTÀ - Based on the designs of Angelo da Orvieto, the building was completed in the second half of the 14C. The architect had been given the task of constructing the building by the Tarlati family of Pietramala.

THE CHURCH OF ST DOMENIC - This imposing building, whose façade has remained incomplete, was finished in the first half of the 15C. The magnificent **interior** has one nave and a cross-beamed ceiling and has been "liberated" of its excessive Baroque decorations. Adjacent to the building is the **Cloister** of a convent (17C), with two orders of arches.

MUNICIPAL PICTURE GALLERY - The gallery is set out in the 16C **Vitelli alla Cannoniera Palace**. The façade of the building is decorated with graffiti by C. Gherardi, with outlines by Vasari. The former artist was also responsible for the decorations, which enliven some of the rooms inside the building. In the portico, some glazed terracottas, bearing the unmistakable features of the work of the Della Robbias, can be seen. The collection of art works on display here lie only second in importance to those of the National Gallery at Perugia.

THE CHURCH OF S. MARIA MAGGIORE - Built between the years spanning the end of the 15C and the beginning of the 16C, the building has a tripartite **interior** divided by brick columns with the coat of arms of the Vitelli family, the patrons who financed the construction of the church.

ALBIZZINI PALACE - The 15C construction merits attention due to its masterly architectural features. A part of the *Burri Collection* is on display inside the palace.

VITELLI A S.EGIDIO PALACE - The construction, which dates from the first half of the 16C, was commissioned by Paolo Vitelli and contains frescoes by Cristoforo Gherardi and Prospero Fontana. At the back of the gardens is the **Vitelli Pavillion**.

THE CHURCH OF ST FRANCIS - The original building, constructed between the 13C and the 14C in pure Gothic style, was altered considerably as a result of Baroque remoulding work (18C). The **interior**, consisting of one nave, has a Latin cross plan with polygonal apses. Worthy of note is the 16C **Vitelli Chapel** designed by Vasari.

THE CHURCH OF THE MADONNA OF THE GRACES - The building, which was brought to completion in the second half of the 16C, has only a few remaining architectural features of the original layout.

ENVIRONS - A little outside the city, in the village of **Garavelle** at the *ex-Capelletti Villa* is the **Museum of The Folk Customs and Artisan Workshops of Umbria**.
The **Spa of Fontecchio** is situated three kilometres from the centre of

Città di Castello, flight of steps and side entrance to the Cathedral

the city. The spa buildings, which were already well known during ancient Roman times, are modern and functional and are located within easy reach of the local amenities and facilities.

The **Parish Church of SS.Cosma and Damiano** stands on the hill of Canoscio. The building dates back to the second half of the 12C. In the 19C **Sanctuary** located on top of the hill, is the venerated image of the *Madonna del Transito* (lit. of death) of the 15C Siennese school.

COLLAZZONE

Typical hill-top village with an evident medieval configuration, Collazzone stands on a hill dominating the point at which the tributaries of the Paglia river flow into the Valtiberina. Most of the village is still encompassed by the turreted castle **walls**.

The **Convent of St Laurence**, formerly a Benedictine abbey, was donated to the episcopacy of Todi and became the convent of the Poor Clares. In the **Crypt**, Iacopone da Todi, who died here in 1306, was buried; later the body was transferred to his native town. The **Parish Church of St Laurence** is located on the site which was once occupied by the highest and most fortified sections of the ancient castle.

COLLEVALENZA DI TODI

Collevalenza is an ancient town which has retained its medieval configuration. Parts of the town are still contained within the encirclement of medieval town walls. It was here, on the splendid fertile hills which provide a magnificent backdrop to the surrounding countryside that several episodes in the life of Madre Speranza Alhama di Gesù (who moved to Collevalenza on the 18th of August 1951) took place. Born in Santomera, near Murcia on the 30th of September 1893, she took her religious vows at the age of 21, joining the order of the *Hijas del Calvario* which, in 1921, became part of *Las Religiosas de enseñanza de Maria Inmaculada*. Later, at the age of 37 she established the *Order of the Sisters of Merciful Love* in Madrid in 1930. In Rome in 1936, the first convent of this religious order was established in Italy and in 1951 the Order of the Brothers of Merciful Love was established. The founding of the Sanctuary of Merciful Love (between 1955 and 1965) brought about great changes to the local econ-

Collevalenza di Todi, the modern Sanctuary of Merciful Love, surrounded by the buildings housing the charity institutions founded by Madre Speranza

omy which is nowadays based on tourism and largely dependent on the visits made by pilgrims and worshipers to the Sanctuary. Madre Speranza (lit. Mother of Hope) died in Collevalenza on the 8th of February 1983 at the age of ninety. After the promulgation of the papal encyclical letter *Dives in Misericordia*, Pope John Paul 11 went on a pilgrimage to the Sanctuary of Merciful Love (1981). A little later, on the 27th of April 1982, the Pope ordained that the Sanctuary be elevated to the rank of Basilica.

The **Sanctuary of Merciful Love** stands on the summit of a hill surrounded by the modern buildings which house the charity institutions founded by Madre Speranza. In front of a wide semi-circular piazza stands a large flight of steps at the base of which is an imposing bell tower that can be seen from miles around. The bell tower was built in such a way as to make sure that the tolling of its bells could be heard from great distances away. Its five bells, clearly visible from the exterior, are dedicated to *Maria SS. del Pilar*, the *Madonna della Speranza*(lit. Madonna of Hope), *S.Giuseppe* (St Joseph), *Maria Mediatrice* (lit. Mary the Mediatress) and to *Amore Misericordioso* (lit. Merciful Love). The embossed copper entrance doors which have beautiful geometric designs and are situated near two large cylindrical sections (the central part of the façade has a cement bay containing a multi-coloured stained glass window depicting the *Crucified Christ*) lead into the spacious hall-like interior. Immediately inside the entrance, marble stoups sustained by rough stone pedestals can be admired. The interior is lit by the bay of the façade and a splendid cone-shaped skylight located in the ceiling of the temple. The concave apse is lit by a bright, multi-coloured stained glass window which runs vertically along the whole length of the building. An interesting feature of the interior is the baldachin (canopy) - a suspended copper crown which is the same size as the high altar and which is an obvious allegorical representation of the crown of thorns which tormented Christ during the Passion. A Paschal candle, carved from elm wood, the pulpits and a tabernacle which stands to the side of the altar (and which has the same architectural features as the Sanctuary itself) are also worthy of note. Of particular interest is the second chapel containing a sculpture of *The Baby Jesus*; the altars dedicated to the *Souls in Purgatory, St Peter and St Paul,* the *Mystery of the Birth of Jesus* as well as the chapels dedicated to *St Theresa of the Baby Jesus* and the *Madonna del Pilar*. The Sanctuary has marvellous acoustics; a magnificent modern organ is situated in the apse. The *Confession Chapel* has simple and yet enchanting modern architectural features. Under the building lies the Crypt which, due to ingenious architectural design, is illuminated by the Sanctuary above it. A part of the building which might almost be defined as a separate lower church is, in actual fact, part of the Sanctuary itself. The mosaic above the altar, dedicated to *Maria Mediatrice*, admirably depicts the *Last Supper of the Virgin and the apostles* and is the work of Mariano Villalta. Outside the Sanctuary, on the right, stands a brick pedestal on top of which is a marble statue of *Maria Mediatrice*. If one faces the Sanctuary one can see, on the right, the **Chapel of Merciful Love**. Constructed in 1955, this was the first part of the complex to be built. In its intimate, serene interior (which has one nave) is a wooden polychrome *Crucifix* carved by Cullot Valera. The mystical atmosphere which pervades the interior is heightened by numerous candles and votive offerings made by pilgrims. A *Way of the Cross* unfolds along the hillside below the Sanctuary; the sculptures located along the various stations of the Cross are the work of Alcide Ticò and Antonio Ranocchia. The charity institutions founded by Madre Speranza include the **Casa della Giovane** (lit. House of Youth) (1962) - the home of the "Sisters of Merciful Love", and the **Institute of Merciful Love**, built in 1953, where members of this religious community live.

COSTACCIARO

A village in the upper Valley of Chiascio situated along the *Via Flaminia,* Costacciaro is an important departure point for excursions into the Regional National Park and particularly to the immense Karst regions (caves) of Mount Cucco.
The origins of the **Church of St Francis** go back to the 13C. The building has a beautiful Romanesque limestone façade.
The **Civic Tower** dates from the 13C and was one of the entrances to the ancient castle. The **Ravelin** is a massive defence structure designed by Francesco di Giorgio Martini.
The excursion to **Mount Cucco** should not be missed as it is an imposing example of the Karst phenomenon in the Umbrian-Marches Apennines. This mountain has a large number of natural caves, including the **Grotta of Mount Cucco** (explorations carried out so far have established that the cave is 922 metres deep and over 27 kilometres in length). Also worthy of note are the Abbeys of **Sitria, S.Emiliano in Congiuntoli**, **Fonte Avellana** (located in the Marches) and the **Hermitage of St Jerome** (recently restored).

DERUTA

Deruta is universally famous for its ceramics and lies to the left of the Tiber, close to Perugia, nestling against the side of a chain of high hills situated between the Chiascio river and the stream of Puglia. Although the first settlements in the district were probably founded during the Eneolithic age, little evidence of the Etruscan presence remains. The first unequivocal references to the place date from the medieval ages and are to be found in an Imperial document in which the town was referred to by the name of *Deruta* (end of 10C). From the 11C onwards, Deruta, whilst still maintaining its autonomous privileges, gradually

Deruta, a panoramic view of the town

came under the domination of Perugia. Having been captured and then burnt to the ground by Braccio Fortebraccio (1408), it was then sacked by "Valentino" (Cesare Borgia). Finally, as a result of the "Salt War" between Perugia and the Pope (1540) the town fell to the Papacy and gained considerable fiscal privileges.

Deruta, which has, in part, managed to retain the highly distinctive features of medieval buildings and town layout, (notwithstanding the disorderly development which has taken place in the more recently founded areas) is certainly the most well-known centre of the region (and beyond) for the production and design of ceramics. The origins of this ancient art go back as far as the Etruscan times, but even before the 14C it was already a well-established and widespread industry, enjoying its heyday during the 16C and 18C. Numerous Italian and foreign museums have pieces of Deruta ceramics on show, including the Victoria and Albert Museum in London and the Louvre in Paris. In particular, mention should be made of the "bianchetto", a kind of white film which is placed over the clay. Designs and outlines are then traced over this before the finished article is glazed. The **Town Hall** is an elegant 14C construction decorated with mullioned windows with two lights. The building, which contains many archaeological and architectural exhibits dating back to both the medieval and Renaissance periods, is the seat of important town institutions including the Picture Gallery and the Ceramics Museum. The **Picture Gallery** contains paintings brought here from the town's churches and numerous works from the *Lione Pascoli Collection*. Amongst the artists whose works are on show here, mention should be made of Baciccia(G.B. Gaulli, *Four Evangelists*); Alunno (N. di Liberatore, *Madonna and Child with Saints*); Fiorenzo di Lorenzo (*Benedictory God above a view of Deruta between S. Rocco and S. Romano*); Guido Reni (*Angel in adoration*); Pieter van Bloemen - known as "Stendardo" (*Ensign, Horses in the stalls*); Placido Costanzi (*S. Francesco di Paola*); Marco Benefial (*St Peter*); and Sebastian Conca (*St Andrew*) and other works by unknown artists of the Umbrian school, dating between the 15C and the 18C, and many other artists. The same building also houses the interesting **Ceramics Museum** which contains 19C-20C local majolica ware, as well as ceramics dating from the 16C and 18C. Worthy of note are some plates, votive tablets, vases, goblets., basins, pharmaceutical containers, fragments of flooring (the one known as *St Francis* is quite famous) and many other exhibits. The beautiful **Church of St Francis** dates back to the second half of the 14C. It has two bell towers, one dating from the 19C, the other built of bricks with elegant mullioned windows with two lights. The interior has one nave, and its lavish Baroque additions have now been removed. Interesting features include a fresco dating back to

Deruta, a ceramist at work in his studio

Deruta: details of ceramics; a kiln for firing terracotta

1420 (*Madonna and Saints*) and fragments of other frescoes dating back to the 14C and 15C. The **Church of St Anthony the Abbot** certainly dates back to before the 15C. Amongst other works, the Church contains interesting frescoes by Bartolomeo (*Madonna of Mercy, and St Francis and S. Bernardino*) and Giovan Battista Caporali (*Scenes from the Life of St Anthony, S.Rocco and St Sebastian*) as well as a glazed terracotta (16C) and an 18C organ. The restored 18C choir is another beautiful feature of the church. Also to be found at Deruta is the **State Institute of Ceramic Art** where students are taught to master the techniques involved in the production, manufacture and decoration of ceramics.

FABRO

The village, situated on a ridge between the Ritorto valley and that of the Chiani, is situated near modern communication networks (the Florence-Rome railway and the "Sole" motorway), a fact which has accelerated its growth and development. In medieval times, Fabro was a feudal possession and thereafter came under the control of Orvieto.
The village has few remaining features of its medieval past. Worthy of note are the remains of the town **walls**, upon which stands a lookout **Tower** built during the first half of the 12C, and the **Parish Church** (19C) with Neo-classical features.

59

Ferentillo, Fortress; in the background, ruins of the medieval walls can be discerned in the surrounding countryside

FERENTILLO

The location of the village, in a narrow gorge of the Valnerina, where the waters of the Precetto run into the river, is a particularly charming one. An early medieval foundation (8C), it was for a long time under the control of the Abbey of San Pietro in Valle. The characteristic features of a medieval village are still largely evident in Ferentillo, thanks to the ruins of the town **walls** and the two **fortresses** dating from the 14C.

Ferentillo is notorious for a large number of mummies, uniquely preserved and discovered in the Crypt of **The Church of St Stephen**. This church is a tripartite Renaissance construction (15C) substantially remoulded during the course of the 18C.

The **Church of St Mary** has frescoes by Jacopo Siculo in its interior and was built around the 13C. Worthy of note, near Ferentillo, is the **Abbey of San Pietro in Valle**, an outstanding example of great architectural and artistic importance. The building we see today is the result of reconstruction work carried out between the 10C and the 12C.

Ferentillo, crypt of the Church of St Stephen containing a large number of mummies

Foligno, a panoramic view of the town and the surrounding Umbrian countryside

FOLIGNO

HISTORICAL BACKGROUND - *An extremely interesting city in the Valle Umbria, it lies to the left of the Topino river, downstream from the confluence of the Menotre, along the plain situated between the Martani Mountains, Mt Aguzzo and Mt Subasio. The origins of Foligno go back to ancient times, when it was known as* Fulginia. *An Umbrian foundation, it then fell into the hands of the Romans at the beginning of the 3C BC., after the battle of Sentino. It was an important centre during Roman times, becoming firstly a* Municipium *and later on a* Praefectura, *undergoing considerable development as a staging post along the* Via Flaminia. *It was converted to Christianity by Feliciano, who became a martyr in 251 AD. Subsequently, it witnessed a period of upheaval and was razed to the ground by the Hungarians and the Saracens. The city flourished under the rule of Barbarossa and grew in both size and importance to become an autonomous commune. Integrated with the territories controlled by the Papacy (beginning of the 13C), it was then taken over by the Imperial forces in 1227, becoming one of the Ghibelline strongholds in Umbria. In 1305, Foligno fell to the Guelph factions led by the Trinci family. It then came under the control of the Papacy once more (except for the Bonaparte interlude) and was finally annexed to the Kingdom of Italy in 1860. Foligno is the birthplace of the architect Giuseppe Piermarini (1734-1808) and had its own school of painters between the 15C and the 16C. Amongst the most famous artists of the Foligno School of Painting are Alunno, Pierantonio Mezzastris, Bartolomeo di Tommaso, Lattanzio di Niccolò, Ugolino di Gisberto, Feliciano de' Muti. The handicraft industries of the region include carpentry, restoration of ancient musical instruments and organ-building. Important folk celebrations held in the town include the* Procession of S.Feliciano *(24 January), the arts festival called* Segni Barocchi *(lit. Baroque features) (during which plays, concerts, films and exhibitions with Baroque themes are held throughout September), and the famous* Giostra della Quintana, *an interesting medieval crossbow contest with a spectacular pageant of historical costumes (second Sunday in September). The typical features of the Roman city are still largely evident in the present-day aspect of the town, as seen by the right-angled shape of the streets and town buildings. The medieval nucleus huddled around the Cathedral, the Town Hall and the Trinci Palace can also be clearly made out.*

61

CATHEDRAL - The Cathedral of Foligno, dedicated to *S.Feliciano* was built in the first half of the 12C on the site where the patron saint of the city was buried. Later extension work (at the beginning of the 13C) led to the building of a second **façade**, which was then enlarged in the 15C and restored during the first decade of the 20C. The front of the building catches the eye due to its elegant architectural characteristics, which are a blend of Romanesque features and Gothic motifs. The most outstanding element is the marvellous Romanesque portal, beautifully decorated with reliefs depicting *Barbarossa* and *Innocenzo III*, the *Symbols of the Evangelists* and the *Signs of the Zodiac*. The elegant dome is a 16C addition built by Giuliano di Baccio d'Agnolo. The **interior** has one nave and betrays the features of Neo-classical remoulding work carried out by Piermarini. It also contains a baldachin,which is obviously a copy of the one in St Peter's, Rome, some paintings dating from the 18C-19C, a silver apotheosis of *S.Feliciano* (18C) and a painting by Alunno. Under the building lies the vast Romanesque **Crypt**.

TOWN HALL - Built around the middle of the 13C, the present day building is the result of numerous transformations carried out over the centuries. It is surmounted by a 15C crenellated tower and has a Neo-classical **façade** (19C), decorated with six robust columns. The **Sala Consiliare** (Council Chamber) is decorated with frescoes by M. Piervittori (end of the 19C).

TRINCI PALACE - Its construction, undertaken during the second half of the 14C, was completed during the first years of the 15C. The **façade** was modified during the Neo-classical period. A striking feature of the building is its large porticoed courtyard, which has a fine Gothic staircase. The interior has many outstanding rooms containing numerous frescoes which date from the 15C and 16C. These include the **Loggia** (*Scenes of the Foundation of Rome*), the **Halls of the Free Arts, the Planets, Human Life, the Emperors and the Giants**. In the passageway, there are portraits of *Famous Characters of Antiquity* and the *Allegories of the Various Ages of Man*. The small **Chapel** contains 15C frescoes by O. Nelli *(Scenes from the Life of the Virgin)*. The ancient home of the medieval nobles houses some of the town's important cultural institutions. The **Picture Gallery** has detached frescoes of the Foligno, Umbrian and Sienese schools as well as works by other schools dating between the 14C and 19C. The most important artists represented here include Alunno and his son Lattanzio, P.A. Mezzastris, B. di Tommaso, B. di Mariotto and B. Gozzoli. In the **Archaeological Museum** are documents and exhibits dating from the Roman age (tombstones, sculptures, reliefs and sarcophagi). The **Town Library** contains numerous volumes as well as a large number of manuscripts and incunabulae (early printed books).

ORATORY OF THE NUNZIATELLA - A typical example of Renaissance architecture, dating from the last years of the 15C. In the interior are two noteworthy frescoes by Pietro Vannucci (Perugino) depicting *The Eternal Father in the act of benediction* and the *Baptism of Christ*. Another interesting feature is a valuable tabernacle in gilded plaster work by Lattanzio di Nicolò, which stands in front of a fresco depicting the *Madonna*.

THE CHURCH OF ST AUGUSTINE - The present building is the result of reconstruction work carried out during the 18C, even if the original building dates from the 13C. Worthy of note are the imposing brick **façade** and a beautiful portal on the right side of the church. In the **interior** is an 18C high altar with wooden carvings, the venerated image of the *Vergine del pianto* (*Weeping Madonna*) and a painting by Felice Damiani, known as the "Veronese" of Umbria.

THE CHURCH OF THE HOLY SAVIOUR - The ancient church (10C-12C) has a rectangular pink and white stone **façade** and three beautiful Gothic portals, the central one being the most outstanding. Another interesting feature is the elegant **bell tower**, which has a spire (14C) and is decorated with lovely mullioned windows with two lights. The **interior**, which underwent significant transformation work during the 18C, contains 16C Flemish tapestries, frescoes and a painted panel by Bartolomeo di Tommaso (sacristy).

Foligno, Cathedral: detail of the beautiful main façade; the second façade looks out over the piazza della Repubblica

THE CHURCH OF ST JAMES - The 13C building was subjected to various transformations during the 15C-17C-18C. Annexed to the Church is the **Convent of the Servants of Mary**, built during the same time as the church itself. The unfinished **façade** (15C) is decorated with two-tone stonework and a delightful Gothic portal. It contains a remarkable painted standard, the work of pupils of Alunno.

THE CHURCH OF ST NICHOLAS - The origins of this church date back to the 14C, even if it later underwent numerous transformations. Worthy of note is a beautiful 16C portal; the **interior** contains two important works by Alunno, depicting *The Nativity, The Resurrection and Saints,* and *The Coronation of the Virgin with Saints.* Other interesting works are contained in the sacristy, where there is also a painted panel by Luca di Tommè.

THE CHURCH OF S. MARIA INFRAPORTAS - This is the oldest church in Foligno and has a 11C portico, which has been transformed in the upper section. The graceful **façade** is characterized by a trilobal mullioned window with two lights; another interesting feature is the square Romanesque **bell tower** (12C). The **interior**, which has an oblong basilica-like plan, is divided into a nave and two aisles. The church contains numerous frescoes by the local school of painters (Alunno, Nelli, Ugolino di Gisberto, Mezzastris). Worthy of note is the **Chapel of Our Lady of the Assumption** (12C) characterized by Byzantine frescoes.

MONASTERY OF ST ANNE AND ST ANTHONY - Also known as the *Monastery of The Countess,* because orders for the construction to be built were given by Beata Angelina of the Marsciano Counts. The Monastery has two remarkable **Cloisters** containing frescoes by Renaissance artists (F. Melanzio, F. de' Muti, L. di Niccolò, P. Mezzastris). In the **Refectory** is a 15C fresco depicting *Scenes from the Life of Christ.* Between the 16C and the 18C, the **Church** of the convent contained the famous *Madonna of Foligno,* counted as being one of Raphael's masterpieces (today it is on display at the Vatican Gallery). Finally, mention should be made of the ex-**Church of St Domenic** (13C, with an outstanding Gothic portal and 14C-15C frescoes); the **Church of**

Foligno, a view of the Church of S. Maria Infraportas

Parts of the Abbey of Sassovivo, near Foligno

S.Giovanni dell'Acqua (lit. of the water), (14C, with frescoes of the same period in the sacristy); the **Church of St Francis** (13C, containing the mortal remains of Beata Angela da Foligno, a 14C mystic).

ENVIRONS - The **Fortress of Sant'Eraclio** was built by the Trinci family at the beginning of the 15C. The walls of the fortress are well preserved and contain two gates and towers. In the small church (with the Trinci coat of arms on the façade) are two frescoes by local artists.

The **Church of S. Maria in Campis** is an Early Christian basilica, enlarged in the mid 15C and reconstructed in the 19C. Numerous finds dating back to Roman times have been discovered in the district, and it is believed that a large settlement was found on this site. It was on this spot that the famous bronze sculpture entitled *Hercules of Foligno* was discovered. In medieval times, the church was known as *S.Maria Maggiore*. In the side chapels are some frescoes of great merit, painted by artists of the Foligno School (Alunno, Mezzastris, Giovanni di Corraduccio). The **Church of S.Giovanni Profiamma** is situated along the ancient *Via Flaminia*, where the *Municipium of Forum Flaminii* stood in Roman times (218 BC.), its name being derived from its founder, a Roman consul. The construction, of harmonious basilica-type features, dates from the 11C-12C and substituted an earlier church built on this spot. The **façade** dating from the first half of the 13C is decorated with a Romanesque portal with reliefs executed by Maestro Filippo. The **interior** has a raised presbytery and a semi-circular apse containing fragments of frescoes (*Madonna of Mercy*). In the **Crypt** there are architectural exhibits dating back to the Early Middle Ages.

The Abbey of Sassovivo stands in a green ilex grove on the slopes of Mt Aguzzo. It was founded in second half of the 11C; it once belonged to the Benedictines of Sassovivo and then passed into the hands of the Olivetani family. The abbey dates back to the 12C, and today it is a popular tourist attraction. A feature of great architectural and artistic interest is the **Cloister** (first half of the 13C), the work of the famous Roman marble sculptor, Pietro de Maria. The splendid marble entablature is supported by round arches resting on 128 double columns. There is a beautiful frieze decorated with mosaics and polychrome marble. Nearby stand the ruins of the **Chapel of Beato Alano** (13C-14C) with an ancient **Crypt**. Thanks to its extraordinary countryside, the **Plain of Colfiorito** is counted as being one of the most interesting naturalist zones in Umbria. The vast plain has been defined as "an area of marshland of international interest". The whole district is renowned for its ornithology, botany and geology. Along the plain stood the ancient pre-Roman settlement of **Plestia**, otherwise known as *Pistia,* and numerous archaeological finds have been discovered here. The ancient **Church of St Mary of Plestia** (10C) was built with left-over Roman building materials.

FORCA CANAPINE

The mountain pass of Forca Canapine can be reached by taking the road which goes from Norcia to Arquata del Tronto. The road runs across the plain of St Scholastica before forking to the left and then winding up through the southern slopes of the Sibillini mountains. The pass, situated at 1541 m, forms the watershed between the river basin gravitating towards the Tyrrhenian Sea and that gravitating towards the Adriatic. It also represents the border between Umbria and the Marches. Situated in the heart of this extremely beautiful stretch of countryside are short-stay tourist facilities as well as the hotels, guest-houses and ski lifts which open during the winter months. This part of the Sibillini mountain range is a favourite spot with both skiers and mountain climbers alike, as it is situated in close proximity to the Piano Grande (lit. Large Plain) and the enchanting hill village of **Castelluccio**. The village is an ideal starting point for excursions into the Sibillini mountains and especially to the highest mountain in this range - **Mt Vettore** (2476 m).

FOSSATO DI VICO

The ancient *Helvillum Vicus* was an Umbrian foundation, allied to Rome. Only a few ruins of the ancient **Fortress**, which once belonged to the nobles of the area, remain standing. This fortified construction was razed to the ground twice during the first half of the 16C. The 14C **Church of St Benedict** is decorated with fine frescoes dating from the 14C and 16C. In the delightful **Church of St Sebastian** is a painting depicting the venerated image of the Virgin Mary, called *Mater Divinae Gratiae.*

FRATTA TODINA

The village is situated on the slopes of a hill which dominates the point at which the Faena stream runs into the Tiber. Its origins probably date back to a settlement which Pliny referred to as *Tudernum*. Fratta Todina, characterized by its **castle walls,** contains the **Parish Church of S.Savino**, built by Giovanni Santini (19C). Nearby stands the 19C **Oratory of St Catherine**. The **Bishop's Palace** is all that remains of the 17C residence, which Cardinal G.B. Altieri commissioned Lodovico Gatteli da Todi to build. A little outside the town stands the **Convent of S.Maria della Spineta**, founded by St Francis. The first stone building dates from the end of the 14C.

GIOVE

A medieval village which also has Renaissance features, Giove is situated on a ridge along a terraced hill which slopes down to the Valtiberina. The imposing structure of the **Ducal Palace** dominates the village. The 16C building was never completed and has Renaissance features built over the most ancient parts of the construction. Nearby stands the **Parish Church**; the elegant façade is divided by pilaster strips and crowned by a semi-circular tympanum, while a fine bell tower rises up at the corner of the building. In the **Chapel of S.Rocco** it is possible to admire the *Crucifixion against the background of Jerusalem,* a 16C fresco by artists of the Foligno school.

GUALDO CATTANEO

A picturesque hill-top village, situated on a hill covered with olive groves, which separates the valley of Puglia from that of the stream of Attone, in the northernmost section of the Martani Mountains. It was founded in the second half of the 10C, even if it would seem that its origins date back to the Roman period. Textiles are still produced by the local handicraft industry. The **Parish Church**, rebuilt in 1804, was constructed in the Romanesque style (second half of the 13C). It contains an interesting crypt and a *Madonna and Child* which dates from the mid 14C. The **fortress** is characterized by a triangular plan and has three interconnecting turreted towers. The **Church of St Augustine** dates from the first half of the 12C. In one of the chapels is a remarkable *Crucifixion*, dating from 1482. Amongst the numerous castles in the surrounding district, one of the most outstanding is that of **S. Terenziano**.

Gualdo Tadino, the robust, turreted Flea Fortress which dominates the surrounding countryside

GUALDO TADINO

HISTORICAL BACKGROUND - *The town, which lies close to the Marches' border, is situated near the Via Flaminia, along the stretch of the foothills of the Apennines dominated by Mt Serra Santa. An Umbrian foundation, it was known as* Tadinum *(or Tadinae) in Roman times, when the inhabited area was situated along the consular road, in the plain located a little to the south of the present day settlement. Since the Romanization of the town (266 BC.) it suffered great upheaval and unrest; it was destroyed by Hannibal (217 BC.), sacked by the partisans of Caesar (49-48 BC.) and was the site of the battle of "Tagina", which resulted in the war between the Goths and the Byzantines. The war was won by the latter (552). It was once again razed to the ground by Otto III (end of the 10C) and was then so badly damaged in a fire that it had to be rebuilt (1237) on the present location. Having become a free commune, under the auspices of Frederick II, it was conquered by the Perugians, before finally coming under the control of the Papacy (second half of the 15C). After* vast *sections of the town were destroyed by an earthquake (1751), it then became part of the Roman Republic during the Napoleonic era. It was then once more assigned to the Church during the post-Napoleonic restoration period and finally annexed to the Kingdom of Italy.*
The present day town is a lively centre of historical and artistic importance, with extremely important monuments and sights. The place is also well-known for its waters, which are low in mineral content and originate from the Rocchetta Springs. It is also universally famous for its ceramic production. The most important folk events and festivals include the Procession of the Dead Christ *(Good Friday); the traditional festivities of* Cantamaggio; *the* International Exhibition/Competition of Ceramics *(August-September); the* Palio delle Porte *("race of the town gate quarters") (last Sunday in September).*

THE CATHEDRAL OF ST BENEDICT - Together with the annexed Benedictine monastery, the Cathedral was constructed by Lombard builders in the second half of the 13C. The church, which has a flight of steps in front of it, has a Gothic **façade** in two orders. The upper order contains a masterly rose window, with oculli on either side; in the lower order are three portals, the central one having exquisite decorative motifs. On the right side of the church stands a beautiful 16C **fountain** by Antonio da Sangallo the Elder. The present day **interior** is the result of 19C remoulding work; it has a nave and two aisles and contains a marble altar-frontal on the 14C high altar. In the **Chapel of Beato Angelo** is a bronze and silver urn containing the mortal remains of Beato.

THE CHURCH OF ST FRANCIS - A Gothic construction dating from the end of the 13C, the church is characterized by the purity of the linear architectural features of its **interior**, which has a particularly outstanding apse. The central nave is decorated with 15C frescoes painted by Matteo da Gualdo. The church also contains the **Picture Gallery**; dominating the collection is a splendid painting of the *Madonna and Saints,* by Alunno, and generally considered to be the artist's masterpiece (1471). There is also a masterly *Annunciation* by Matteo da Gualdo, other painted panels, frescoes painted by various schools, works by Antonio da Fabriano, Sano di Pietro, Avanzino Nucci, a *Cross* painted by an unknown Umbrian artist of the 13C and a multicoloured ceramic altar-piece.

THE FLEA FORTRESS - The turreted bulk of the fortress is a distinctive feature of the hill on which it stands and which, in turn, dominates the town below. Considered to be one of the most important examples of medieval military architecture, its name is derived from Fleo, a small water course which flows nearby. The fortress, which was restored many times during the period of Papal domination, houses the **Town Archives**. These contain important documents, dating back to the 13C and 18C, land registers, several deeds, proclamations and edicts. Particularly important documents include the lyrical laud-book (or hymn book) of the Raccomandati di Maria (a religious order) and a liturgical manuscript.

TOWN HALL - A relatively recent construction (18C) which replaced the pre-existing Palace of the Guilds and Priors, which had been built at the beginning of the 14C and was then razed to the ground by the earthquake of 1751.

CIVIC TOWER - Also known as the *Rocca Minore* (the smaller fortress), it was built in the 13C and was restored after it partly collapsed (during the earthquake which struck Gualdo around the middle of the 18C) and after the construction of the Baroque lantern, which surmounts the tower.

ENVIRONS - The **Church of the Holy Trinity** is situated in a solitary and evocative spot, just under the summit of Mount Serra Santa. Commonly known as the *Hermitage of Serra Santa*, it once contained a ceramic altar-piece (16C) believed to be by Monina del Gualdo. Today this can be seen in the Picture Gallery of the chief town of the province. Since remote times, the mountain has provided shelter for hermits and anchorites, who found refuge for meditating in the numerous caves and hermitages, which, according to legend, were also visited by St Francis.

GUARDEA

The modern town has replaced the ancient settlement (Guardea Vecchia), which was situated up in the hills and abandoned as a result of the incessant damage caused by frequent landslides. It has been ascertained that the origins of the *castrum* of Guardea date back to the days of Germanic domination. There are very few remains of the ancient **Guardege**; the crumbling ruins of a tower (12C), and the ruins of fortifications keep vigil over the underlying plain. Other ruins dating back to medieval times can be seen in the **Rione Marruto** (Marruto District). The **Castello del Poggio** (lit. Hill Castle) has the characteristic layout of a medieval village enclosed within its town walls. The **Parish Church** is an 18C construction which has an urn containing the mortal remains of Beato Pascuccio. The **Cave of St Francis** is annexed to an 11C *Camaldolite Monastery.* Nearby stands the *Church of S. Illuminata.*

Gubbio, a panoramic view

GUBBIO

HISTORICAL BACKGROUND - *Gubbio is an ancient, noble city, majestically spread out along the foothills of Mt Ingino. The Saonda river runs right across the large, wide plain which stretches out below the city. The Carmignano river and one of its tributaries (which are, in turn, both tributaries of the Saonda river) run through the city. The whole area is framed by green, undulating hills and mountains. Even if the first settlements of the district around Gubbio seem to date back to pre-historic times, we are at least certain that Gubbio was founded by the Umbrians and that it soon became both a meeting point and the scene of confrontation between these and the nearby Etruscan civilization, as testified by the* Eugubine Tablets. *These constitute an important key to the understanding of the civilization and language of the Umbrians, as well as providing insight into the structure of this city-state between the 3C and IC BC. The seven bronze slabs, written partly in the Umbrian alphabet (derived from the Etruscan one) and partly in bastardised Latin, are a significant historical record of exceptional value. These unique bronze slabs were discovered during the middle of the 15C underneath the Roman amphitheatre. Each slab is inscribed on both sides and, as well as providing historians with important information about the ceremonies which took place in the ancient city, they are also a source of information and descriptions of the district. For example, it has become clear that first important Eugubine settlement was made up of two separate communities: the* Arce Fisia *and the* Tota Ikuvina *located at different altitudes along the slopes of Mt Ingino. The first community was located higher up on a spot which had commanding views of the underlying city and a large part of the plain stretching out towards the horizon; the second settlement defended by walls with three main gates was situated lower down. Close scrutiny and analysis of the bronze slabs has also revealed that the Romanization of the Eugubine territories was, at least in the initial phase, a relatively peaceful and amicable episode in the city's history. During this early phase, elements of the ancient, indigenous Umbrian traditions were maintained alongside innovations introduced by the Roman laws and administration. It was only at a later date, after the IC AD. that the ancient Eugubine civilization was forced to comply with the*

69

canons of the Latinity, especially as regards religious matters. The Romanization of Gubbio dates from 295 BC. In that year, during the battle between the Romans and the Etruscans, Umbrians and the Gauls at Sentino, Gubbio did not fight alongside their traditional enemies - the Etruscans. As a result of the city's decision to refrain from fighting against the Romans, it was granted a treaty which later led to its being granted Roman citizenship (Iguvium), included within the Crustumina tribe, and rewarded for not having fought in the rebellions which the Italian confederates carried out at Corfino (90 BC.) The decline of the Roman Empire led to the destruction of Gubbio during the Gothic War (5C). In the 8C the city fell to the Lombard kings Liutprando, Astolfo and Desiderio. With the development of free communes (11C), Gubbio grew in importance, a fact which immediately led to bitter conflicts with the town of Perugia. The free communes rapidly collapsed and soon a series of bloody, armed battles took place (1151, 1183, 1216, 1217, 1258 and 1259). Meanwhile the political necessities of the Germanic emperors led to firstly, Frederick 1 of Swabia and later Henry V1 and Otto 1V to ratify Gubbio's territorial acquisitions and annul an onerous peace treaty imposed by the citizens of Perugia. Towards the end of the century the Guelphs took over the control of the city and a period of relative peace and stability ensued. A Ghibelline attempt to overthrow the city was soon nipped in the bud (1300). Around the middle of the century Giovanni di Cantuccio Gabrielli took control of the city. However his early demise led to Gubbio being taken over by the Church. Meanwhile external conflicts and the disintegration of the social fabric of the city paved the way for the Counts of Montefeltro to gain control, thereby establishing Gubbio as a possession of Urbino, and subsequently part of the Papal States (1624). After the Napoleonic Wars and the short-lived Roman Republic, the city became part of the new united State on the 14th of September 1860.

As a city of cultural and historical traditions, Gubbio has an exceptional wealth of artistic and monumental heritage. The layout of the town centre is steeped in the characteristic features of medieval buildings and streets, creating an interesting environment, which also includes marvellous examples of Renaissance architecture. The widespread use of limestone confers warm chromatic tones upon the buildings of the town, whilst towers and palaces intermingle with Gothic churches and the austere façades of residences and houses, which have over the years acquired a charming characteristic patina. The town plan of Gubbio betrays the characteristic configuration of medieval centres still enclosed within town walls. At the same time, both the centre and outlying areas have adapted to modern living conditions. The city is the birthplace of the miniaturist Oderisi (13C), the painter Ottaviano Nelli (15C), the ceramist Giorgio Andreoli (Maestro Giorgio 15-16C) and the architect Matteo di Giovannello (The Gattapone, 14C). If tourism, together with agriculture and industry are important factors of the city's economy, the contributions made by the local handicraft industry should not be overlooked. This secondary concern involves the production and manufacture of ceramics, together with wrought iron work, carpentry and copperware. The local cuisine is characterized by wholesome home-made dishes, whilst the white truffle is an appetizing accompaniment to both autumnal and winter fare. Amongst the local festivals, which blend elements of both the sacred and profane, in this religiously important city (it was the scene of many important episodes in the life of St Francis), mention should be made of the Procession of the Dead Christ (Good Friday); the Corsa dei Ceri ("Candle"/Tower Shrines Race) held on 15th May; the Palio della Balestra (Crossbow Competition) (last Sunday in May). From the middle of July until the middle of August Classical Plays are also put on at the Roman Theatre.

The "Corsa dei Ceri" deserves special mention. Due to its religious and secular connotations, and the exuberant atmosphere it engenders, the "Corsa dei Ceri" can be said to be on a par with the famous Palio of Siena. On the 15th May, the eve of the patron saint's day (S. Ubaldo) Gubbio cheers on the "ceraioli" (candle makers/bearers), represented by the ancient town corporations, which carry enormous polygonal wooden towers, topped with a wax saint (Ubaldo, George and Anthony the Abbot) on their shoulders. The lively "race" finishes at the Basilica of S.Ubaldo on Mt Ingino. This tradition, which is perhaps incorrectly defined as a "race" (because it is not a competition, seeing that S. Ubaldo must always arrive at the Basilica first), is linked (according to one of many hypotheses) to an episode in medieval history. It is supposed to commemorate the day on which the Eugubines,

Gubbio, the Palio della Balestra and the traditional Corsa dei Ceri

with the help of Ubaldo, fought back a confederation of rival communes who had surrounded the town. The event is also rooted in pagan ritual, harking back to expiatory rites and favourable auspices at the advent of the spring.

During the Christmas festivities, a gigantic and phantasmagorical Christmas "tree", swathed with hundreds of lights and neons, illuminates the slopes of Mt Ingino, creating a magical, enchanting effect.

71

On the opposite page: Gubbio, a view of the surrounding countryside dominated by the Consuls' Palace; above: typical local ceramics with the Consuls' Palace

CONSULS'PALACE - PALACE OF THE PODESTÀ - These two architecturally associated buildings look out over *Piazza Grande,* a "hanging" piazza par excellence (so-called because it occupies a ledge of the hill). The piazza constitutes the architectural and monumental heart of the city. The charming architectural and monumental proportions of these two buildings, their simple elegance, the symmetrical proportions of the windswept piazza, "invented" in the 14C, constitute some of the most outstanding focal points of the town. These features anticipate architectural themes, which would find mature expression a century later in the Florentine Renaissance.

Both palaces date from the 14C and were designed by the Eugubine architect Matteo di Giovannello, better known as Gattapone. The magnificent Gothic portal, (which has a flight of steps in front of it) set in the **façade** of the Consuls' Palace, is by Angelo da Orvieto. The façade itself is divided vertically by pilaster strips, with a series of small jutting arches along the top, which are crowned with merlons - a feature repeated in the turreted tower dominating the building. The palace, also known as *Palazzo dei Popolo* (People's Palace), was once the seat of the highest magistracy of the Commune; the building also houses the **Picture Gallery** and the **Archaeological Museum**. In the Gallery are paintings by artists of Gubbio dating from the 14C to the 16C, paintings by the Venetian school, a *Madonna of Mercy* by an artist of Perugia, and a 16C *St Francis* by A. Sacchi. The most outstanding exhibit in the Archaeological Museum is the *Eugubine Tablets*, which constitute a unique key to both the understanding of the ancient Umbrian language and civilization and the study of the ancient Italic populations. Other exhibits on show include archaeological finds, ceramics and coins. The Palace of the Podestà, also known as the *Magisterial Palace*, is the seat of the local town council. Along the northern side of the piazza stands the **Ranghiasci-Brancaleoni Palace**, the only Neo-classical building in Gubbio.

DUCAL PALACE - Masterly example of Renaissance architecture in the city, the palace was built at the behest of the Duke of Urbino, Frederick of Montefeltro sometime after 1470, on the site of a Lombard palace. The building, which contains a splendid internal courtyard, partly surrounded by porticoes, was in all probability designed by Francesco Laurana, even if it is not certain whether he actually supervised its construction, which was probably completed by Francesco di Giorgio Martini. Inside the building some of the ancient furnishings are still to be found, although, as the property has changed hands many times, most of these have now been sold off.

CATHEDRAL - The present day building dates from the last twenty years of the 12C, when the ancient Roman town was abandoned in favour of the safety of the slopes of Mt Ingino. The **façade** is characterized by a beautiful pointed portal and a large circular window, decorated around the edge with *Reliefs of the Evangelists*. In the **interior** which has a Latin cross plan consisting of one nave, the ceiling is supported by enormous pointed arches. It also contains numerous paintings and frescoes of 16C Umbrian artists. In the presbytery are two organs by the local engravers L. and G. Maffei (16C). Annexed to the Cathedral is the **Diocesan Museum** which contains 14C-15C painted panels, detached 15C frescoes, an ivory *Crucifix*, a valuable 16C cope and other interesting objects and exhibits.

THE CHURCH OF THE MASONS - The church is also known as the Church of *St Francis of Peace* because, according to legend, it was built on the site of where, one night, St Francis tamed a wild wolf. It was built at the beginning of the 17C and entrusted to the University of Stone-Masons and associated guilds. In the **interior** one can admire three statues depicting *S.Ubaldo, St George* and *St Anthony*, which during the "Corsa dei Ceri" (15 May) are placed on top of three large wooden towers.

THE CHURCH OF ST MARZIALE - In ancient times, the church was also known as that of *St Andrew*, and this denomination was given to an entire town district up until 13C. An erudite clergyman of the 19C put forward the hypothesis that the Church was originally a pagan temple consecrated to the God of War. The modern day building, which forms part of the **Convent of S.Marziale**, has the characteristic features of the Late-Romanesque period and also has a small bellcote.

VEHIA GATE - It is the last surviving town gate of ancient *Iguvium*, which can be admired today. The Romans called it the *Janea Gate*, but over the centuries it was referred to by many other names. Today it is more well-known as the *Arch of S.Marziale*, due to its proximity to the church bearing the same name. The enormous square blocks of stone used in the construction of the arch and the lateral supports give an idea of the powerful dimensions, which the ancient town walls must have had. It dates back to between the 4C and the 3C BC.

THE CHURCH OF S. MARIA NUOVA - A 13C construction with decidedly harmonious Cistercian features, the Church was, in all probability, built on the site of a pagan temple consecrated to Janus. The **façade** has elegant and linear features. The **interior** contains a fresco dating from 1413, depicting a *Madonna of the Belvedere*. This painting is generally considered to be the masterpiece of the Eugubine artist Ottaviano Nelli. Other valuable works include an *Annunciation* by the 14C Umbrian artist, Guido Palmerucci. The so-called *S.Ubaldo's coffin* has two busts of *Saints* by the expressionist Maestro of S.Chiara.

THE CHURCH OF ST AUGUSTINE - The 13C Church has a brick **façade** dating from the beginning of the 20C. The **interior**, which has one nave, is characterized by transversal arches which support the ceiling. The apse contains frescoes by O. Nelli depicting, in 26 episodes, *The Life of St Augustine* and *Universal Judgement*. The annexed **Convent** was built during the same period; it was built on land donated by the Commune.

THE CHURCH OF ST PETER - Although the date of its construction has still not been ascertained, the church is known to have been consecrated in 1058. Re-utilized ancient architectural features, which are particu-

Gubbio, a view of the Ducal Palace and the apse of the Cathedral

larly evident in the **façade** (the remains of four columns with Corinthian capitals in the Byzantine style, some small corbels with animal and floral motifs), would suggest that a more ancient church once existed on the site of the present one. In all probability, this church was part of the Benedictine abbey which existed here up until the 7C. At the beginning of the 16C, the monastery became a possession of the Olivetani family, who enlarged the church and held on to the control of the complex until the mid 19C. The monumental and symmetrical proportions of the **interior** betray the transformations carried out during the Renaissance. The church contains a beautiful 13C wooden *Crucifix*, some fine frescoes by Raffaellino del Colle and artists of the Caravaggio school and a valuable Baroque organ, exquisitely carved by Maffei (1598).

THE CHURCH OF THE VITTORINA - In front of the Church is a *Monument to St.Francis* taming the wolf. The building has ancient 13C origins, and some architectural features dating from those times are still visible. It was reconstructed in the 16C and takes its name from the locality in which it is situated. This locality was once known as *Vetturina*, (appearing as such on a town map of the 19C), probably derived from *Vehia Turena*, an ancient settlement which existed on this spot. The fame of this Eugibine church is connected to the popular story,in which St Francis tamed a wild wolf. According to legend, this episode is said to have occurred near the small church.

THE CHURCH OF ST FRANCIS - The original building dates from the second half of the 13C and was designed by Fra' Bevignate (although this theory is much disputed). The bare **façade** has a Gothic portal and a small rose window. To the side of the tripartite apse stands an octagonal **Bell tower**. In the **interior**, which has one nave and two aisles (it is the only church in Gubbio to have this internal division), traces of the 18C restructuring and remodelling work can be seen. The left chapel has frescoes depicting the *Story of the Virgin* by O. Nelli; other 15C paintings depict the *Virgin and Child with St Christopher and St Anthony the Abbot*. The right chapel has fragments of 14C frescoes and, under the vault, *Christ the Redeemer* and the *Evangelists.* An outstanding feature of the annexed **Convent** is the restored **Cloister**.

LOGGE DEI TIRATORI (WOOL FACTORY) - The building, whose correct name is really Loggia dei Tiratori, is the upper section of a 14C church. Its construction at the behest of the Wool Merchants was undertaken in the 17C. Almost at the end of the portico, on the left, is the **Bianchi Church**, annexed to a hospital bearing the same name. This was once decorated with frescoes and paintings, which have now for the most part been detached and removed to the Diocesan Museum.

BENI PALACE - Masterly 15C construction, which belonged to the family of the Beni counts, who also gave hospitality to two popes here. Some of the rooms had frescoes by Ottaviano Nelli (first half of the 15C). Today, unfortunately, the remaining frescoes are very badly preserved. Some frescoes, which were detached from the main hall towards the end of the 19C, are now part of the *Cagnola alla Gazzada Collection* near Varese.

THE CHURCH OF ST DOMENIC - The existence of this ancient place of worship once dedicated to *St Martin*, has been known since the 12C. Having been taken over by the Domenican Order (14C), it was then enlarged. However, the building we see today is the result of remoulding work carried out during the second half of the 18C. The **interior** in the shape of a Latin cross, contains 15C frescoes by pupils of Nelli. The fourth chapel on the left contains a masterly terracotta *Pietà* (15C). Behind the high altar is a lectern with beautiful carvings attributed to Terzuolo.

CAPTAIN OF THE PEOPLE'S PALACE - This 13C construction, characterized by pleasant architectural features, most probably belonged to the Gabrielli family. The popular belief that says that it belonged to the Captain of the People has not been historically verified. Inside the building a most unusual **Museum of Torture Instruments Used Throughout the Centuries** has been laid out.

Gubbio, the interior of the Church of St Francis and a view of the Captain of the People's Palace, which houses the Museum of Torture Instruments Used Throughout the Centuries

BARGELLO PALACE - The 13C building is characterized in the lower section of its façade by an elegant window. Its name is derived from the "Bargello" (or magistrate), an official of the free commune. During this era, the building was the combined police station and governor's office.

THE HOUSE OF S. UBALDO - The 14C house is generally believed to have been the birthplace of S.Ubaldo (1084-1160). Even if the actual building (which has the salient features of a noble Eugubine house) cannot, chronologically speaking, possibly be the one in which Ubaldo Baldassini was born - it seems to have been ascertained that the building did belong to his family.

THE CHURCH OF ST JOHN - This building, which was reconstructed in the 13C on the site of an ancient baptistery, has an elegant Romanesque **façade** with a wide Gothic portal surmounted by an oculus; at the side of the building stands a beautiful bell tower. The **interior** has one central nave and contains the customary transversal arches supporting its ceiling - a feature which is evidently derived from Gothic-Cistercian architecture.

THE CHURCH OF S. SECONDO - The origins of this church are extremely ancient; documentary evidence has shown that this was once the administrative seat of the Church of Ravenna in Gubbio (6C-8C). In the present day building, later transformations carried out over the centuries can be seen. The apse, which has recently been restored, has pleasant 13C linear features. The **interior** contains some 15C-17C frescoes.

ROMAN AMPHITHEATRE - The theatre at Gubbio is counted as being amongst the largest and best-preserved in Italy. Some parts of the construction would seem to suggest that it was built in the Republican period; built of rough ashlar stones, some of its features were created using the *opus quadratum* technique. The **Cavea** (70 metres in diameter) is divided up into four wedge-shaped sections by flights of steps. During the summer months plays and classical drama are put on here., The theatre also has a proscenium (stage) and an orchestra pit, whilst an inscription, discovered in the second half of the 19C, gives details about the existence of two basilicas restored by the quadrumvir Gneus Satrius (1C AD.).

MAUSOLEUM - This large aristocratic tomb dates back to Roman times. The burial chamber is well preserved, even though the external walls are almost totally ruined. According to Tito Livio (Tito Livius or Livy), the mausoleum is the tomb of Gentiius, King of the Illyrians, which was won in 168 BC. and given in custody, with the family, to the inhabitants of Gubbio. Another hypothesis, however, believes that it is the tomb of a certain Pomponius Gricinus or Grecinus.

THE CHURCH OF THE MADONNA DEL PRATO - Built in the second half of the 17C, it is characterized by its simple and yet refined Baroque-style features. The **interior** contains fine frescoes by F. Allegrini *(Assumption of the Virgin, Mercy, Martyrdom of St Stephen, Paradise, Faith, Charity);* G Lapis *(S.Francesco di Paola);* L Dorigny *(Baptism of Christ, S.Ubaldo, Hope).*
Almost at the summit of Mt Ingino (827 metres in height), which can either be reached by car or cable car, stands the **Basilica of S.Ubaldo.** The construction of the present church, built at the behest of the Governing Lateran Canons (ecclesiastical councils), dates from the 16C. Sources suggest that prior to this date another small church. containing the remains of S.Ubaldo (transferred here in 1194), once stood on this site. Outstanding features include the beautifully decorated portals and the **Cloister** through which one enters the Church.
The **interior** is divided into a nave and four aisles and is lit up by large windows decorated with *Scenes from the Life of S.Ubaldo;* worthy of note are the engraved marble altar and the glass urn containing the perfectly preserved body of the patron saint. Finally, it should also be remembered that the traditional "Corsa dei Ceri" (candle/tower shrine race) finishes at this spot. The three large wooden towers used in the"race" are on display throughout the year in the first aisle on the right of the church.

A view of the shores of Lake Trasimeno

LAKE TRASIMENO

In terms of dimension, Lake Trasimeno is the fourth largest lake in Italy. It is situated in the province of Perugia and is the biggest stretch of water on the Italian peninsular. It has a surface area of almost 128 kms, reaches a maximum depth of 6.55 metres and has a perimeter of 54 kms. Formed as a residual lake of an ancient and vast basin situated in the Valdichiana, the width of the lake has altered considerably over the centuries, being in fact dependent on the seasonal and cyclic trend of the rainfall. The problem of regulating its waters has existed as far back as the Roman and medieval times, and it was only in 1423, under Braccio Fortebraccio of Montone, a nobleman of Perugia, that the so-called **Vecchio Esautore** (lit. one deprived of authority) was built. This consisted of an artificial drain which, by means of an underground network of canals and tunnels, allowed the excess waters to be drained off. When deprived of a natural outlet, the excess waters would cause widespread and devastating flooding along the riverside territories, causing great damage to crops. From 1423 up to the beginning of the 17C, various popes had to supervise the periodic maintenance and servicing of the drainage system. At the end of the 19C, the construction of a new drainage tunnel brought an end to the age-old problems, which the Vecchio Esautore had never completely managed to resolve. In more recent times, the occurrence of long periods of drought has led to a fall in the level of the waters and an abnormal increase in algae. As a remedy to this worrying phenomenon, which puts both the existence of the lake itself and the life of numerous aquatic species in jeopardy, the streams of Rio Maggiore and Tresa have been artificially deviated into the lake. Lake Trasimeno, in all its resplendent beauty, lies surrounded on three sides by a backdrop of gently undulating hills, covered with olive groves and Mediterranean scrub. On the side facing towards Tuscany, a wide open plain stretches out. Three islands emerge out of the calm waters of the lake: the **Polvese** (the largest in terms of dimension), the **Maggiore** (the most populated) and the **Minore** (the smallest, uninhabited island). The territory of Trasimeno was inhabited since Etruscan times, as numerous tombs discovered around the hills of Castiglione and Città della Pieve have testified. Later, the area around the Lake came under Roman domination, and here the Romans were subjected to one of the most disastrous defeats in their military history. On 23rd June, 217 BC., during the course of the second Punic War, the Carthaginian army fought against the Roman soldiers on the northern shores of the lake. The Carthaginians, led by Hannibal, wiped out the Roman army led by the Consul Flaminius, who was killed in battle. In the Early Middle Ages, the territories were donated by Otto I to the Papacy. Perugia and Florence fought over its possession, before it later became disputed over by the Church and the Grand Duchy of Tuscany. Between 1797 and 1798, Trasimeno gave its name to a district of the Roman Republic, while between 1809 and 1815, the lake gave its name to one of the districts of the Empire created by Napoleon Bonaparte. Today, the dense conglomeration of fortified hill villages, the rocks, the castles, the fortifications and the towers remind us that the area of Trasimeno has always been a contested frontier.

Castiglione del Lago

The largest resort in the tourist district of Trasimeno, Castiglione stands on a calcareous promontory covered with olive groves, near the western shores of the lake. A fertile alluvial plain stretches out behind Castiglione. The formation of the alluvium dates back to the time when once the waters of the largest basin on the Italian peninsular completely surrounded the promontory, creating the fourth island of Trasimeno. The first people to inhabit the land were the Etruscans who, according to Pliny, were defeated by the nearby population of Chiusi. Pliny, in fact, always referred to the locality as *Clusium Novum*. Evidence of an ancient Etruscan colony on the site where Castiglione del Lago stands today is also provided by the considerable number of Etruscan tombs dotted throughout the region. The area was also populated during Roman times. Due to its advantageous strategic position and for its fertile soil, Castiglione was long disputed over by the dominating powers. During the Early Middle Ages, it belonged to the abbots of S.Gennaro di Campoleone, before passing into the hands of the people of Perugia, who made it into a fortified defensive stronghold (12C). For a long time, it was contested by the towns of Arezzo, Orvieto and Cortona. It then fell to the Della Corgna dukes, under which it became a marquisate from the middle of the 16C to the middle of the 17C. In the meantime, Pope Paul V transformed it into a duchy, and it then became integrated into the State of the Church (18C). Today, Castiglione is a popular tourist and holiday resort, which has a wide range of accommodation facilities. The lively town centre, for the most part still encompassed within the medieval town walls, and the flourishing handicraft industry (lace and fishing nets), together with local festivities like the *Tulip Festival* (April) and the *Kite Festival* "Let's colour the skies" (25/4-1/5), biennial) make the town one of the jewels of the enchanting chain of hill centres situated along the shores of the lake. Castiglione's role as the small "capital" of the Trasimeno area is especially evident during the summer months when tourists come here to take the ferries to the islands of the lake (the Provincial Administration of Perugia runs regular services to Isola Maggiore and other riverside locations). It also has a large beach with excellent bathing facilities. Traditional agricultural activities, local businesses and a thriving industrial sector also contribute to the economy of the region.

The **Castle** was built by Frederick II of Swabia and rises up over the town, offering good views of the lake. The polygonal castle walls are crowned with merlons and have alternating round and square towers. The high central keep has a triangular plan. In the vast inner gardens an open air theatre has been set up where plays and concerts are held during the summer. The castle was once known as the *Castle of the Lion* and its impregnability was a source of great interest to Leonardo da Vinci. According to some experts, the present day name of this riverside town is probably derived from the castle's former name.

The **Ducal Palace**, the seat of the present Town Council, was originally built as a tower-house by the Baglioni counts of Perugia. At the beginning of the 16C, Giampaolo Baglioni gave hospitality to Machiavelli and Leonardo da Vinci here. Leonardo designed plans for a new revolutionary drainage system for the territories lying between Trasimeno, the Valdichiana, the Valdarno and the Valtiberina. In the second half of the 16C, Ascanio Della Corgna transformed the building into the Ducal

Castiglione del Lago, an aerial view and the rounds along the embattlements of the Castle

Palace we see today, based on plans by either Vignola or Alessi. A covered passageway, now partly ruined, connected the palace to the castle. The construction, which is regarded as being one of the most masterly examples of Renaissance architecture in Umbria, has interesting frescoed rooms painted by G.A. Pandolfi and S.Savini (second half of the 16C).

The present day **Church of St Mary Magdalene** is the result of transformation work carried out in the 19C. It has a Neo-classical façade; in the interior, which has a Greek cross plan, is a *Madonna del Latte* (14C) and a painting believed to be by Eusebio da S.Giorgio and pupils (16C) depicting *The Virgin and Child with St Anthony the Abbot and Mary Magdalene.*

The **Church of St Domenic** is the result of 18C reconstruction work and contains *The Tomb of the Della Corgna family.* The building has an interesting lacunar ceiling.

The boat excursion to the **Island of Polvese** is well worth the trip. The largest of the islands of Trasimeno (54 hectares), it is part of the province of Perugia, which has declared it a protected area, in order to safeguard and encourage the growth of species of aquatic plants. In ancient times, it was under the rule of Perugia, and a community of Olivetan monks lived here. Among the tourist attractions are the ruins of a 13C **Fortress** and the remains of a **Monastery**. The *Provincial Navigational Service* runs boat trips to **Isola Maggiore** (cf Passignano sul Trasimeno).

Lisciano Niccone

A hill-top village situated in the upper valley of the Niccone stream (a tributary of the Tiber) on the right bank of the river. The first human settlements in the area date back to Etruscan times. Important remains of the Etruscans include the fortified seat of Bellona near the summit of Mt Murlo and the hypogeum of Villa Sagraia. The origins of the place-name Lisciano seem to date back to Roman times and are a reference to *Lisius* (or *Licius*), who owned some territories here. As a matter of interest, the Niccone stream marked the border between the Grand Duchy of Tuscany and the Papal State.

In July the **Festival of Bringolo** (a local gastronomic speciality) is held. Interesting tourist attractions include the ruins of **Lisciano, Reschio, Pierle** and **Sorbello** castles, the churches of **St Nicholas, St Thomas** and **S. Maria delle Corti**.

81

Magione, a view of the Castle of the Knights of Malta with its characteristic round turreted towers

Magione

A charming medieval village, which stands in an isolated setting along a gentle hilly ridge. One side of the ridge descends down to the eastern shores of Lake Trasimeno, whilst the other side dominates the plain of Pian di Carpine. The first reliable documentary evidence relating to a *Villa of Pian di Carpine* dates back to medieval times. In the second half of the 14C, the Knights (of the Order) of St John of Jerusalem founded Magione di Pian di Carpine on the site of a 12C Benedictine abbey. Magione is probably derived from *Mansio* (a place where horses were kept in Roman times) and in time, came to be the place name of the present village.

The locality has a thriving handicraft industry, which is known for its production of wrought iron, copperware and the preparation of fishing nets. Local festivities include the celebrations of *Jubilee of the Holy Crucifix* (held every twenty five years, the next one will be held in the year 2001), the feast day of *St Clement* (23rd November), Carnival and the *Segalavecchia* (satirical folk songs) half way through Lent.

The **Castle of the Knights of Malta**, also known as *Badia (Abbey)* has bastions, towers and round turreted towers. The present day construction is the result of 15C reconstruction work, carried out by Fieravante Fieravanti of Bologna. The existence of the **Church of St Mary of the Graces** also known as *Madonna dell'Ospedale* has been ascertained since 1209. Reconstructed and enlarged (first half of the 17C), it has an 18C bell tower, built on the site of an ancient look-out tower The ancient **Lombard Tower**, part of which lies in ruins, was once known as the *Tower of Pian di Carpine.*

The **Parish Church of St John the Baptist** is the result of construction work carried out between the 17C and 19C. The interior contains a 17C wooden *Crucifix*, which every twenty five years is carried through the village during the *Jubilee* celebrations. In the surrounding district of Magione, interesting sights include the fortified village of **Montecolognola** (end of the 13C), the ruins of the **Monte del Lago Castle** and the **Sanctuary of S.Maria del Soccorso** (18C).

Panicale

An enchanting hill-top village, situated along the hills, which encompass the southern district of the "amphitheatre" of Lake Trasimeno. Panicale is characterized by the elliptical configuration of its medieval village, which is still enclosed within the encirclement of its ancient walls. The enchanting serenity of this hilly landscape, which seems like the background to one of Perugino's canvas and the magnificent panoramic

Panicale, a panoramic view of the medieval centre

views over the nearby lake, make Panicale a popular tourist attraction and an ideal spot for relaxing holidays. The first references to the place are contained in a document signed by Berengario (10C). In medieval times, Panicale was a stronghold of the city of Perugia, which had fully appreciated its important strategic position. In the 16C-17C, it was sacked by the armies of Valentino (Cesare Borgia) and those of the Farnese nobles. Recently its importance has declined in favour of the market town of Tavernelle.

Embroidery work and wrought iron are the main handicraft industries of the locality. Local festivities include the *Procession of the Dead Christ* and the *Fiaccolata di Pasqua* (Easter) (a torch-lit procession). The local saint's day of *St Michael the Archangel (*29 September) is also a local festival.

The *Piazza Umberto I* is characterized by a fountain and by the **Magisterial Palace**, the façade of which is decorated by civic coats of arms.

The **Collegiate Church of St Michael** looks out over the piazza bearing the same name and has two stone portals. In the interior is a *Nativity* by Caporali. The **Palace of the Podestà**, characterized by a mullioned window with two lights, dominates the village.

Outside the walls stands the **Church of St Sebastian**, which contains two masterly frescoes by Perugino: *The Martyrdom of St Sebastian* and *The Coronation of the Virgin*.

Nearby, close to Tavernelle, is the Renaissance **Sanctuary of the Madonna of Mongiovino**. The construction has a central plan (16C) and is crowned with an eight-sided cupola. It also has two portals, carved by Rocco di Tommaso da Vicenza and other artists. The interior contains a high altar by Francesco di Alessandro da Fiesole and frescoes by Arrigo Fiammingo and Niccolò Circignani, better known as " Il Pomarancio".

Passignano sul Trasimeno

A small jewel of a town set along the northern shores of Trasimeno. The locality is divided into two parts. The more ancient medieval part of the town lies on the slopes of a small ridge facing towards the lake, while the more modern part of the town stretches out along the shores of the largest lake basin of the Italian peninsular. It was a place of transit even in remote times (a fact that would explain the origins of the modern place name) and was both an Etruscan and Roman centre, as well as a Byzantine stronghold during the Gothic War. It was annexed to the Marquisate of Tuscany by Charlemagne and referred to as *Castrum Passiniani* by Berengario (10C). At the turn of the 12C, the locality had exerted its influence over most of the northern territories. Having been seized by Perugia, which built important fortifications to combat the

Passignano sul Trasimeno: view of the medieval centre and the lake-front; the small jetty of Trasimeno

rival armies of Arezzo, it was then subjected to serious retaliations in which the town suffered both considerable damage and loss of life.

Under Bonaparte, it once again became extremely important in administrative terms, when it was made the seat of the District of Trasimeno, whose jurisdiction extended as far as the neighbouring Communes, with the exception of Castiglione del Lago. The locality was subjected to repeated air raids during the Second World War.

Passignano sul Trasimeno is nowadays a popular holiday attraction and a well-known bathing resort. The economy of the locality is largely based on tourism, although the ancient fishing and ironwork industries are also thriving activities. Local folk events include the *Palio delle Barche* (Boat Race), an age-old traditional event, which takes place on the last Sunday in July.

The town, which is dominated by the ruins of the **Fortress** has ancient towers (one of which has a clock), steep medieval streets and pointed Gothic gates.

In the **Church of St Christopher**, once known as the *Parish Church of St Mary of Passignano* (13C) one can see fine votive frescoes painted by 15C Umbrian artists.

Worthy of note are the **Church of S.Rocco** (Renaissance) and that of **S.Bernardino**, which has a typical Umbrian sandstone façade (15C). In the outlying district stands the 16C Church of the **Madonna dell'Uliveto**, which has architectural features reminiscent of the work of Bramante. In the interior is a 17C holy-water font believed to be the work of pupils of Ascanio da Cortona, and a fresco of the *Madonna and Angels* by Caporali. Also of interest is the marvellous Corinthian high altar by the 16C artist Mariotto Radi. The **Church of St Francis** situated just below the *Parco della Rimembranza* is also worth visiting. From this pleasant setting among the hills running along the northern side of the lake, fine,sweeping views of the northern shores of Lake Trasinmeno can be enjoyed.

Castel Rigone, an enchanting village situated in a beautiful panoramic setting (Rigonella Park) is well worth visiting. Interesting features of the area also include the ruins of the 13C **Castle** and the beautiful **Church of the Madonna of Miracles** - a fine example of Umbrian-Renaissance architecture. The absidal construction, has a Greek cross lay-out and an adjoining bell tower and was built by Lombard builders at the turn of the 15C. The façade is decorated with a 16C portal and a rose window. Masterly 16C frescoes by Berardo di Girolamo Rosselli and G.B. Caporali are to be seen in the interior. The bell tower which stands to the side of the church dates back to the beginning of the 19C. The original bell tower which had much finer architectural features collapsed during an earthquake.

From the port of Passignano, the navigational services of Trasimeno run enjoyable excursions to **Isola Maggiore**. The second most important island of Trasimeno has a serene and idyllic atmosphere and a compact size. In the pretty island village, women still carry on the traditional craft of lace making, producing beautiful examples of Irish lace. In 1211 St Francis spent a period of fasting on the island (the episode is commemorated by a bronze *Statue of the Saint*). In the **Church of the Holy Saviour** (13C) is a *Virgin and Child* by Sano di Pietro; in the **Church of St Michael the Archangel** is a painting by G.B. Caporali (Crucifixion) situated at the altar. The frescoes decorating the cross vaults of the presbytery are also by G.B.Caporali. Parts of these frescoes depicting the *Four Evangelists* and some *Heads of Saints* are attributed to an Umbrian artist who was influenced by the painting of Benozzo Gozzoli. The church, built in the Umbrian Gothic style, dates from the middle of the 14C. Along the main road of the village stand numerous 16C buildings such as the **Bartocci** and **Squarti** palaces. In the highest part of the island stands the Villa Guglielmi - a castle-shaped building and the 13C **Church of St Francis**. The **Isola Minore**, which lies opposite (now deserted) was once inhabited by fishermen and hermits. Here, the ruins of the **Church of S.Mustiola** can be seen.

Tuoro sul Trasimeno

Pleasantly located near the hills which run along the northern side of the lake, the locality is set in a splendid scenic landscape. Even though its origins are relatively modern (14C), its fame is rooted in the memorable battle fought out between the Romans and the Carthaginian army (217 BC.).
In the **Capra Palace**, a masterly piece of architecture, interesting archaeological exhibits are on display, several of which date back to the famous battle of Trasimeno.
The **Parish Church of St Mary Magdalene** stands on the site of where the Church of S.Agatha once stood. The church was once part of the Abbey of S.Maria di Farneta (13C) and later became part of the Abbey of Pieve Confini.
On the outskirts of Tuoro, the **History of the Battle** is illustrated on stone slabs (which depict interesting historical, archaeological and scenic details of the Battle of Trasimeno). Another feature is the **Campo del Sole** (lit. Field of the Sun).

LUGNANO IN TEVERINA

An enchanting medieval village, which stands in an isolated position on the summit of a hillock facing the Valtiberina, in the western part of the Amerini hill range. It was founded in the 7C.
The **Farnese-Ridolfi Palace** dominates the village and is known locally as *Pennone* (pole), as it is reminiscent of a ship's mast.
The **Collegiate Church of Our Lady of the Assumption** is one of the most elegant Romanesque buildings in Umbria. Built in the 12C, on the site of an ancient 11C church, it has a pronaos which was added to the building in the first half of the 13C. The interior has beautiful Cosmatesque flooring which extends as far as the base of the altar. In the crypt is a venerated 15C alabaster *Crucifix.* The apse has a 15C tryptych by Alunno, depicting *Madonna and Child with Saints*, as well as a *Crucifixion* in the style of Giotto and a 16C *Beheading of St John the Baptist* by Livio Agresti.

MARSCIANO

A large town in the district of Todi, situated on the right of the Nestore river, just before the point at which this runs into the Tiber. The first references to the place are contained in a document dating from the first years of the 11C.
Local handicrafts produced here include manufactured cloth, costumes and masks. The **Parish Church**, a Neo-Gothic building, has a 19C Neo-classical bell tower. The interior contains a fresco (16C) by the school of Perugino. Worthy of mention are the **medieval walls**, upon which stand the turreted **Castle of S.Apollinare** and the so-called **Bulgarelli Tower**

crowned by merlons supported by corbels, with an adjoining portico.
Amongst the numerous picturesque villages in the district, mention should be made of **Cerqueto**, whose **Parish Church** contains a *Crucifixion* by Tiberio d'Assisi and a *St Sebastian,* the first known work attributed to Perugino (1478).

MASSA MARTANA

The locality stretches out along the foothills of Mt Martano. It seems certain that the first human settlements in the place date back to the second half of the 3C BC. The **Parish Church** dedicated to *S.Felice* contains the holy relic of the *Sacred Thorn.*
The encirclement of ancient **town walls** dates back to the late 10C and includes many sections of later reconstruction work. In the so-called **Castle Gate** are some plaques and epigraphs and a coat of arms of the Fonzi nobles. The **Fonnaia Bridge**, built of mighty stone blocks, is one of the most magnificent testimonies to the Roman presence in the town. Nearby the ruins of some **Spa buildings**, constructed during the reign of Tiberius, have been discovered. The **Catacombs** (2C AD.), known for a long time as the *Traiana Cave*, are a burial place consisting of three corridors in the shape of a Greek cross. The **Church of S.Maria in Pantano** was built on the site of a pagan temple of the ancient *Vicus Martis.*
Another building in the district of the chief town of the commune is the **Church of St Mary of Peace** (16C).
Along the ancient *Via Flaminia* stands the 15C **Church of St Mary of the Graces** characterized by a masterly rose window set in the simple stone façade. In the district of Massa Martana stands the ancient **Church of S.Illuminata**, a building which dates back to the year 1000.
The **Church of S.Pietro sopra le Acque** (lit. above the waters) is situated in a pleasant woody spot, which has a wealth of natural water resources. The **Abbey of S.Faustino** has a modern travertine bell tower in front of it, which is built in the Romanesque style. The ancient church is situated on a spot which was already sacred in Roman times.
The **Abbey of S.Fidenzio and S.Terenzio** has ancient origins (in the 11C, the Benedictine abbey was annexed to it).

MONTE CASTELLO DI VIBIO

An interesting hill village of the Todi district, situated above the spot where the Faena stream runs into the Tiber.
The Teatro (theatre) della Concordia is the most evident testimony of the splendour achieved under Bonaparte (beginning of the 19C).
The Parish Church of St Mary of Miracles was completely rebuilt in the first half of the 19C. The **Church of S.Lorenzo in Vibiata** has the typical features of the Romanesque-Ravenna style of architecture and was built between the 11C and 12C.

MONTECASTRILLI

The small villages of this commune of Amerino are dotted along the green undulating hills. The strange place name seems to be derived from *Castrillorum*, the small encampments set up in the area by Hannibal during his march towards Rome.
The chief town is characterized by its elliptical shape and by its distinctive medieval features. The prime activity of the local handicraft industry is the manufacture of artistic ironware, while the most characteristic festival is the *Market/Exhibition of Agricultural Machinery and Poultry* (last ten days in April).
The **Parish Church** has a beautiful 15C wooden *Crucifix* and some 17C frescoes. The **Convent of the Poor Clares** (16C) has windows which betray the typical motifs of the Byzantine style.
In the silence of the surrounding countryside, there are some important architectural buildings: these include the ancient **Small Church of S.Lorenzo in Nifili**, a pretty construction dating back to the year 1000 and the so-called **Caesar's Fort**, a group of abandoned farmhouses on the site of ancient Byzantine defence castles.

Montefalco, the original Renaissance façade of the Church of S. Illuminata and the Gate of Frederick II

MONTEFALCO

The ancient small town, which by virtue of its enviable position on a fertile hill, (dominating the Valle Umbra, Foligno and the point at which the Clitunno river runs into the Tiber) has been nicknamed the balcony of Umbria. It is an interesting artistic centre, characterized by distinctive medieval features and beautiful elegant buildings.

It was already a thriving locality in Roman times (it is probably the ancient seat of *Mons Faliscus* -destroyed during the 1C BC. after the civil wars) and was converted to Christianity by S.Fortunato around the 4C. Known as *Coccurione* during the Middle Ages, it was then razed to the ground by Frederick II (1249) and, after being re-built, was given the present place name. With the setting up of the free communes (14C), it became the seat of the court of the Duchy of Spoleto. Conquered by the Trinci family (1383), after a period of upheaval and destruction, it was then handed over to Baldino di Niccolò Maruzzi by the Papal authority, before being taken over by the Church (1446). Numerous losses were incurred as a result of an epidemic of plague and the sacking of the locality by the armies of Orazio Baglioni (16C). It was thereafter made a town in 1848.

The local handicraft industry still manufactures cloth, while local festivities include the *Procession of Christ Arisen* (Easter Saturday), the local patron saint's day *S.Fortunato* (1st June), the *Festival of St Clare of Montefalco* (17 August) with the *Torch-lit Procession* (on the evening of 16 August), and the *Fuga del Bove* (lit. Escape of the Ox) which brings an end to the festivities of August.

Most parts of the medieval town of Montefalco are still enclosed within the encirclement of the **town walls**. These date back to the 14C and are surmounted by towers. The town gates are set within the walls. Rising up above the town stands the **Tower of St Augustine**, which is connected to a town gate bearing the same name. It is characterized by its jutting upper section, which is supported by corbels and crowned with Ghibelline crenellations along the top. Other town gates include the **Gate of Frederick II**, the **Camiano Gate** and the ancient **Fortress Gate**, demolished at the beginning of this century.

The **Church of St Francis** which was de-consecrated in the middle of the 19C, today contains an important **Museum and Picture Gallery**. It is a

Montefalco, the Sanctuary of the Madonna of the Star

14C construction, with a Renaissance portal set within its modern façade. It has a large, wide nave and a ceiling with wooden cross beams. On the right side is an aisle, added at a later date. Amongst the important art works are the splendid frescoes by Benozzo Gozzoli in the central apse *(Episodes from the life of St Francis, Scenes from the Life of St Jerome and Saints);* the chapels containing frescoes by Giovanni di Corraduccio (15C); canvases by Fantino di Bevagna (Ascensidonio Spacca); the niche containing frescoes by Perugino *(Nativity, The Eternal Life, Annunciation)*, a fresco by Tiberio d'Assisi *(Enthroned Virgin and Child with Saints)* and other works by Alunno, F. Melanzio, Antoniazzo Romano, Pier Antonio Mezzastris and others.

The **Church of St Augustine** was constructed in the years between the second half of the 13C and the first half of the 14C. The façade is decorated by a beautiful pointed portal; the interior, consisting of two aisles contains important frescoes in the Umbrian-Siennese style. Some of the artists represented here include Domenico Alfani, Ugolino di Gisberto, P. Mezzastris and G.B. Caporali.

The **Church of St Clare**, which contains the remains of St Clare of Montefalco in its interior (an eminent figure of Umbrian mysticism who lived between the 13C-14C), is a Baroque construction, remoulded in the 17C. In the **Chapel of S.Croce** are fine 14C frescoes by Umbrian artists. Near to the Church is the Augustinian **Convent** which has a cloister (15C).

The **Church of S.Illuminata** was built on the site of a pre-existing place of worship, at the turn of the 16C. The building, which contains motifs of the Lombard-Renaissance style in its interesting brick façade, contains some fine 16C frescoes, painted by Francesco Melanzio and Bernardino Mezzastris of Foligno.

Other churches worthy of note are those of **S.Maria di Piazza**, containing a 16C fresco by Melanzio; **S.Leonardo** (paintings by Melanzio and J. Vincioli); **S.Lucia** (12C) and **St Mary Magdalene** (13C, transformed in the 18C).

The **Town Hall** (13C) has few remaining parts of the original building; the loggia on the ground floor is a later 15C addition.

Other 15C-17C buildings include the **Langeli Palace** (once known as the *Tempestivi* Palace); the **Moriconi-Calvi Palace**; the **Santi-Gentili Palace**; the **De Cuppis Palace**; the **Senili Palace** (also formerly known as the *Tempestivi Palace)*.

A little outside the town is the interesting convent of **S.Fortunato**. Its origins date back to the 4C-5C, even if the building as it stands today is the result of 15C reconstruction work. In the beautiful four-sided portico are some Roman columns built from re-cycled building materials. The portal is decorated with a fresco by Benozzo Gozzoli, who also painted the

S.Fortunato and the *Virgin and Child* which can be admired in the interior. The interesting Chapel of the Rose has 16C frescoes by Tiberio d'Assisi. Again, in the outskirts of Montefalco stands the **Church of S.Maria di Turrita** (frescoes dating from the 14C-16C); the **Sanctuary of the Madonna of the Star** (19C paintings by artists from Rome, Livorno, Naples and Perugia) and the fortified medieval village of **Fabbri**.

MONTEFRANCO

Picturesque village situated on a mountain ridge in a pleasant and scenic setting, above the lower part of the valley of the Nera River. Probably a Lombard centre, it was for a long time governed by the Duchy of Spoleto. Amongst the local festivities, mention should be made of the celebrations which take place in May to commemorate *S. Bernardino.* The village contains ruins dating back to medieval times., the most important being the ancient **walls** and **gates** which are connected to an ancient fortress. The **Church of the Cemetery** contains 17C frescoes.

MONTELEONE DI SPOLETO

A hill-top village situated on the left side of the upper valley of the river Corno, a tributary of the Nera, close to the Regional National Park and the Lazio border.
An ancient proto-Italic seat, it was first known as *Trebula Metusca* and then as *Trebulanus* in Roman times. In 1902 a tumulus (barrel-shaped) tomb, containing a wooden two wheeled chariot (or wagon) embossed with laminated bronze, was discovered in the district. The object, which is believed to be of Ionian origin, dates back to 6 BC. and has been classified as Etruscan by leading experts. The exhibit now forms part of a collection on display at the *Metropolitan Museum of Art,* New York.
The village, is noted for its production of ceramics and its excellent "farro" (farley/spelt), which has grown here since Roman times. The local festivities include two religious festivals: the *Festival of the Cross* (3 May) and the *Festival of the Madonna of Mercy* (first Sunday in September).
The **Church of St Francis** is a beautiful 14C-15C Romanesque-Gothic construction. Nearby stands the **Clock Tower**, a feature which is all that remains of the ancient manor-house. The main road of the village is lined with buildings of great architectural merit. Worthy of note are the **Town Hall** (formerly the *Rotondi Palace*), 16C; the **Church of St John the Baptist**, whose façade has a 15C coat of arms and a stone carving of a *Sacrificial Lamb*; the **Congiunti Palace** (16C) and the beautiful **Bernabò Palace** (15C).
The presnt day **Parish Church** is the result of reconstruction work carried out in the second half of the 18C. In the small village of **Ruscio**, near the Corno river, stands the **Church of S.Maria del Piano**, which has extremely ancient origins and was once known around the year one thousand as *S.Maria de Equo.*

MONTE SANTA MARIA TIBERINA

An enchanting medieval village, situated in an isolated position above the valleys of the Tiber and the Aggia stream. The origins of the settlement would seem to date back to Etruscan times.
When in season, exquisite culinary specialities based on truffles and mushrooms can be tasted here. Local festivities include the *Procession of the Madonna,* which takes place on Ascension Day.
The village has retained many important medieval features, which are particularly visible in the encirclement of its **walls**. The **Bourbon Palace** (masterly portal) still contains a curious feature - "La buca per lettere anonime" (lit. the letter box for anonymous letters).
The **Parish Church** has extremely ancient origins; two outstanding features include the **Chapel-Burial Chamber of the Bourbons of Monte**, enclosed by an artistic 16C wrought iron railing and two sandstone sarcophagi. In the small village of **Lippiano** stands the mighty **Castle**, an imposing stone construction which lies partly in ruins.

MONTONE

The village of Montone stretches out along a green hilly ridge, situated between the Lana and Cárpina streams, which are both tributaries of the Tiber. The origins of the village would seem to date back to a village fortified by the Umbrians, which was also a thriving centre during Roman times. Since the 13C, Montone's history has been intrinsically linked to that of Perugia by an act of spontaneous submission. The noble family of Fortebraccio originates from this area. Later the family moved to the city of Perugia, where Andrea Braccio (1-7-1368) was born, a figure who was to play an important part both in the history of the city and Umbria itself. Local festivities include the *Festival of the Relic of the Holy Thorn* (Easter Monday), the commemoration of the *Arrival of the Holy Thorn* (the week before the "Ferragosto" - a mid-August Bank holiday) with a historical pageant, and the patron saint's day of *S.Albertino* (3 September). The **Church of St Francis** is a masterly example of 14C Gothic architecture. One outstanding feature is a splendid 16C inlaid main portal. The interior has a nave and a polygonal apse and contains such a wide range of excellent artworks, that the Church has now become a small museum (*Town Museum*). The walls are decorated with votive frescoes painted by unknown artists. At the first altar on the left is a painting by G.B. Caporali (15C) depicting *St Anthony of Padua with Seraphim, John the Baptist, Raphael the Archangel and Tobiolo*. On the right is another work by Caporali, the *Madonna dell'Aiuto* (lit. of help), even though some sources attribute this painting to Bonfigli. Also worthy of note are a masterly *Calvary* (Crucifix), a valuable Romanesque-Umbrian (13C) work in polychrome wood; a 16C inlaid bench and the choir with beautiful choir-stalls. Annexed to the building is a delightful 16C **Cloister** with a double portico. The **Collegiate Church**, dating from the first half of the 14C was reconstructed in the second half of the 17C. The building has a Latin cross plan, a circular apse and contains a gilded lacunar ceiling. The church, which contains the venerated relic of the Holy Thorn, also has paintings by Parenti and pupils of Perugino.
Also worthy of note are the ancient **Parish Church of St Gregory** (11C); the ruins of the **Baccio Fortress** and near the town the ruins of the **Aries Fortress**.

NARNI

Narni is an important industrial town in the district of Terni. It is situated on a calcareous rocky ridge, covered with olive groves, below which lies the plain of the river Nera. Under Roman rule it was known as *Narnia* and was a strategic centre and flourishing *Municipium*.
Local festivities include the *Tournament of the Rings*, a kind of medieval tournament in costume dress (second Sunday in May). The town also hosts the *Theatre Festival of the Town of Narni* (last ten days in June).
The centre of the medieval town is the characteristic *Piazza dei Priori* (Priors' Square), the site of a beautiful polygonal **Fountain**. Overlooking the square is the elegant **Town Hall** (13C); the present day building is an amalgamation of three tower-houses. Amongst the rooms situated in the interior is the Town Council Chamber which contains paintings by Ghirlandaio and Spagna. Opposite this building stand the imposing arcades of the **Loggia dei Priori** (Priors' Loggia). Dominating the Loggia is the bare and robust **Civic Tower**.
The **Cathedral of S.Giovanale** is a beautiful Romanesque construction (1145), which was later enlarged and transformed. The simple façade has a 15C portico, decorated with a beautiful frieze. Dominating the whole building is an imposing brick and stone bell tower. The interior, which has one nave and two aisles, has a frescoed Gothic apse and an additional aisle, which was built in the 15C. Outstanding features include two wooden pulpits decorated with reliefs by the Comacini masters.
Dominating the town is the **Fortress**, built in the second half of the 14C, inspired by Albornoz and constructed by Ugolino di Montemarte, probably helped by Gattapone. The square shaped building is dominated by robust corner towers and a high keep.
The **Church of St Augustine**, a 15C construction, has a bare façade with a portal, at the side of which is a fresco by Antoniazzo Romano. The in-

Narni, a panoramic view of the town which dominates the plain of the river Nera

terior, with one nave and two aisles, contains a *Crucifix and Saints* by pupils of Antoniazzo Romano, 16C frescoes by Torresani, a *Virgin and Saints* (15C) attributed to Matteo d'Amelia and a wooden 16C *Crucifix;* the dividing arches of the nave and aisles are similar to those of the portico. The **Church of St Francis** is a 14C Gothic construction originally a small oratory, which was part of a Franciscan convent. It has a fine portal with an aedicule; the interior, which has a nave and two aisles, contains masterly 14C-15C frescoes.

The **Church of St Domenic**, a 12C Romanesque construction, has now been turned into a museum. The façade has a beautiful decorated portal; the imposing Romanesque bell tower is also an interesting feature. The interior, consisting of one nave and two aisles, contains an *Annunciation* by Benozzo Gozzoli; the *bust of S.Bernardino*; a valuable terracotta by Vecchietta; a fresco by Matteo d'Amelia *(Madonna and Saints)*, a chapel frescoed by the Zuccaro brothers, and a 15C marble tabernacle, attributed to Agostino di Duccio.

A little outside the town, at the Nera river, stands the robust arch of **The**

Narni, one of the sides of the Cathedral of S. Giovenale and the façade of the Town Hall which has masterly Romanesque bas-reliefs

Narni, view of the Fortress, with keep and corner towers

Bridge of Augustus. This arch, which is the only one of four arches to have survived, is built of travertine blocks and is the most important remaining feature of Roman Narni. The beginning of "via delle acque" (lit. the road of the waters) (*Via Tiberina)* was once situated near the bridge. **CONVENT OF THE SACRED CAVE** - It is worth making an excursion to the Convent founded by St Francis of Assisi in the 13C. The building, which is located in a pleasant setting amongst ilex groves and chestnut trees, was transformed by S.Bernardino in the 15C.

NOCERA UMBRA

An important town in the upper valley of the Topino River, Nocera Umbra stretches out along a hilly ridge situated between the Subasio river and the Apennine mountains of Mt Pennino and Mt Acuto. The district of Nocera has been inhabited since the Neolithic era, but it was the Umbrians who built the first village here, which was called *Nukeria* (or *Noukria* meaning "new fortress"). Colonized by the Romans, who named it *Nuceria,* it then acquired the title of *Municipium* (municipality) and was an important staging post along the Via Flaminia. References to the town can be found in the writings of Ptolemy, Pliny the Elder and Strabo. It was razed to the ground during the time of the barbarian invasions. Having been acquired by the Lombards (6C), it then became a fortress and a stronghold under the Dukes of Spoleto. As a result of the spreading of Christianity, Nocera was soon elevated to an Episcopal seat, and became a free commune during the 12C. At the beginning of the 13C it was taken over by Perugia, and towards the middle of the century. It was razed to the ground by the soldiers of Frederick II. It then became a fief of the Trinci family and formed part of the lands under Papal domination. Since the 17C, Nocera has been a popular holiday resort and a spa town (because of its mineral water).

The modern town of Nocera Umbra has a thriving ceramics industry, an artisan tradition which has been handed down since ancient times. The place is also famous for its thermal waters. Local festivities include the patron saint's day of *S.Rinaldo* (9 February), the *Festival of the Waters* (August) and the *Horse Race of Satriano* (September).

The **Campanaccio**, also known as the *Trinci Tower,* is the last remaining feature of the fortress of Nocera. The turreted building, which has a square-shaped plan, is in actual fact a bell tower, its origins dating back to the 11C.

Nearby, in a position dominating the town, stands the **Cathedral**, which, over the years, was subjected to several reconstructions. It was originally built in the Romanesque period (11C), although few sections of the original building remain. It was then destroyed by Frederick II. After having been rebuilt (15C), it was then damaged by earthquakes and restored in the Neo-classical style towards the end of the 18C. In its interior, which has one nave and side chapels, lie the mortal remains of the Bishop S.Rinaldo. The Chapel of the Madonna is decorated with stucco work by Francesco Silva di Morbio and with paintings by Giulio Cesare Angeli.

The **Church of St Francis** has a beautiful rectangular stone façade, decorated with two portals, one of which is clearly Gothic in style (pointed and trilobate). The building houses the **Town Picture Gallery**. The collections, including archaeological exhibits dating from the Palaeolithic era to the Renaissance period, contain frescoes by Matteo da Gualdo and works by various artists. Amongst the most important are paintings by Niccolò Alunno (*Nativity of Christ, Coronation of The Virgin*) and a *Madonna and Child* by Segna di Bonaventura. Finally, there is also a masterly *Crucifixion with Virgin and Saints* (13C) by pupils of Maestro di S.Francesco and fragments of *The Funeral Monument of Bishop Favorino*, a 16C work by artists from the workshop of Rocco da Vicenza.

Also worthy of note is the **Old Gate** (once the gate of *St Francis*), the only one remaining of three town gates which were once situated in the encirclement of the medieval walls; the Byzantine **Palombara Tower**, and the churches of **St Philip** built in the Neo-Gothic style by Luigi Poletti (19C), the Romanesque **St Clare**, with paintings by C. Maratta (17C) and **St John**, Romanesque in origin and once known as *S.Maria Antica*.

Near the town, some interesting buildings include the **Baths of Nocera**, a holiday and spa resort dating back to the 17C, and the **Church of Bagnara**, with fragments of 15C-16C frescoes. This church is famous for an episode in the life of St Francis, which took place here and is celebrated annually in the Horse Race of Satriano. The episode refers to when St Francis, who was taken ill in this area, was taken home by horsemen from Assisi, so that he would not die outside his native town.

Nocera Umbra, a panoramic view

Norcia: the robust Castellina fortress designed by Vignola, with its sloping corner towers and a view of the Town Hall

NORCIA

HISTORICAL BACKGROUND - *In mystical, artistic and monumental terms, Norcia is a very interesting city, spreading out along the edge of the Plain of St Scholastica, crowned by the Apennine mountains, which culminate in the scenic ramparts of the Sibillini Mts. Probably a centre founded by the Etruscans, which was also inhabited by the Umbrians and the Sabines, it was mentioned in the works of famous poets and Latin writers (Virgil and Cicero). A small compact 19C town, which has a considerable number of medieval ruins, the whole of Norcia is enclosed within the 14C town walls.*

THE BASILICA OF ST BENEDICT - Its construction was undertaken during the late 13C on the site, where the house of the patron saint's parents is believed to have stood. The white **façade** in the Umbrian Gothic style, has a sloping roof, with corner spires and a magnificent central rose window. In the middle of the façade stands a masterly Gothic portal, which is exquisitely decorated. In the lunette is a fresco depicting *Madonna and Child with Angels*. On each side of the lunette are exquisite small Gothic aedicules containing sculptures of *St Benedict* and *St Scholastica*. Above, *Figures of the Evangelists* surround the rose window. Annexed to the side of the building is the small portico "delle misure" (lit. of the measures). At the end of this stands the late 14C **Bell tower**. The **interior** which contains 18C reconstruction work has a central nave and is in the form of a Latin Cross. Paintings include *St Benedict and Totila*, attributed to Filippo Napoletano (Filippo di Liagno of Norcia, 17C); the *Resurrection of Lazarus* by M. Carducci; the *Madonna and Child, St Scholastica and Saints* by V Manenti. The **Crypt**, which contains features of Roman masonry and 14C frescoes, is probably all that remains of a pre-Romanesque place of worship, built over the birthplace of St Benedict.

CASTELLINA - An imposing 16C fortress, it was built to plans by Vignola. It is a square-shaped construction with robust, sloping corner towers. In the courtyard is a four-sided portico with a double loggia. The **Civic-Diocesan Museum** is located inside the building.

TOWN HALL - The present day building is the result of several reconstructions. The portico on the ground floor is all that remains of the most ancient part of the construction (13C). The upper part of the **façade** has Neo-classical features designed in the second half of the 19C by D. Mollaioli of Perugia. The adjoining **Bell Tower** stands on a 17C flight of steps and was reconstructed in the 18C. Some of the most important rooms in the interior include the **Council Chamber** with a 16C altar-frontal by Jacopo Siculo (*Coronation of the Virgin)* and the **Sala dei Quaranta** whose walls are lined with 18C tapestries depicting the *Four Continents*. Finally, also to be seen in the **Priors' Chapel** is the reliquary of St Benedict, a fine example of Gothic-Renaissance gold carving (16C).

CATHEDRAL OF S. MARIA ARGENTEA - Like most of the buildings in Norcia, the Cathedral stands in the immediate vicinity of *Piazza St Benedict* (the heart of the town and probably the site of the Roman Forum, which contains the *Monument to St Benedict* by F. Prinzi of Palermo (19C)). The construction dates back to the 16C, after a pre-existing Church had been dismantled, in order for the Castellina to be built. The **façade**, built by Lombard masons, has a portal with a small porch (an arch sustained by columns) and a large central oculus; at the side of the building stands an imposing **Bell tower**. Along the side of the church is another beautiful Gothic portal. The **interior** of the present church (it has been rebuilt several times) is the result of 18C reconstructions carried out by Maggi and has a nave with two aisles and a polygonal presbytery.

THE CHURCH OF ST AUGUSTINE - Once dedicated to *St Agatha*, it is a 14C construction and its **façade** is decorated with an elegant Gothic splayed portal and a lunette containing a fresco. The **interior**, which has one central nave, contains an exquisite 17C wooden choir and some 15C-16C paintings, including the *Virgin and Child with Saints*, believed to be by Ansovino da Camerino, and *S.Rocco with St Sebastian and St Barbara* attributed to pupils of Spagna.

ORATORY OF S. AGOSTINO MINORE - Also known as *S. Agostinuccio* (lit. the young Augustine), it is believed to have been built on the site of an ancient pagan temple consecrated to Mars. The valuable collection of furnishings contained here make it one of the most interesting buildings in Norcia. The splendid panelled ceiling, with exquisite gilt decorations, is further enhanced by sculptures of *St Mary, St Augustine, St Benedict* and *St Scholastica.* Also worthy of note are the walnut choir stalls (16C) and an inlaid and engraved solid walnut altar dating from the same period.

THE CHURCH OF THE CRUCIFIX - A 15C building, which was restored in the 18C. It contains a hall-shaped **interior**. The beautiful 15C wooden *Crucifix*, which gives its name to the church, is located above the high altar, which also contains a travertine *Funeral Monument.* Also to be seen are tapestries depicting *The Betrayal of Judas* and *Jesus in the Praetorium.*

THE CHURCH OF ST JOHN - The origins of this church date back to the 14C, although it has undergone many reconstructions, as can be seen from the **façade**, the appearance of which was altered significantly after an earthquake damaged the structure at the beginning of the 18C. The **interior** divided into two aisles, contains two interesting 16C frescoes (*Madonna del Cardellino,* (lit. *Madonna of the Goldfinch)* and *Virgin and Child with St Benedict and St Scholastica).* The 18C lacunar ceiling is also an outstanding feature.

AEDICULE - This is the name given to a small temple, formerly known as *La Maina*, built in the second half of the 14C by Vanni Tuzi and beautifully decorated with delicate bas-reliefs. The small square building has a travertine facing.

THE CHURCH OF ST FRANCIS - A splendid ashlar stone construction dating from the second half of the 14C. It has a beautiful splayed Gothic portal with a lunette containing a fresco, and a masterly rose window in the upper part of the **façade**. The **interior** has one nave and contains parts of the ancient pointed vault. Among the remaining frescoes are those depicting the *Virgin and Child Enthroned with Saints* and *The Transfiguration of St Anthony of Padua.*

ENVIRONS - At the foot of the picturesque "Mountains of the Sibyl" stands the small charming village of **Castelluccio**, situated on a pyramid-shaped relief at 1452 metres. It is in a pleasant position dominating the Pian Grande (Large Plain). The locality is an ideal starting out point for excursions towards Mt Vettore (2476 metres), the highest peak of the Sibillini Mountains and the underlying **Lake of Pilate**.
The **Abbey of S.Eutizio** was founded, according to legend, by the patron saint in the late 5C. The beautiful 12C Romanesque church survives to this day and is dominated by a 17C bell tower.

Norcia, the Umbrian Gothic façade of the Basilica of St Benedict, opposite the Town Hall

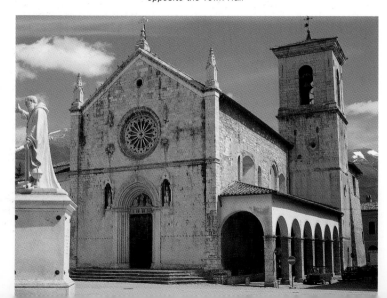

Orvieto, a panoramic view of the city and its famous rugged rocks

ORVIETO

HISTORICAL BACKGROUND - *An enchanting city situated close to the border with Lazio, Orvieto rises up on a crag of tufa emerging from the serene profile of the Umbrian hills, dominated by the spectacular Maitani mountains. The territory of Orvieto has been populated since remote times, even if its first known inhabitants were the Etruscans, whose presence here is marked by a considerable amount of archaeological remains (the Necropolises of the Cannicella and the Tufa Crucifix). Even though there are few known facts about the Etruscan* Volsinii, *it has been clearly ascertained that it was destroyed by the Romans (first half of the IIIC BC.). Having been colonized by the Romans, the natural communication networks of roads and rivers were exploited, to the detriment of the town itself, which in the meantime came to be known as* Urbs Vetus *(the old city). Between the 3C and the 4C, the river port of Pagliano, situated at the confluence of the Tiber and Paglia rivers, grew in importance. With the decline of the Roman Empire, Orvieto was also subjected to the inevitable spate of Barbarian invasions. Having been seized by the Goths and then conquered by the Byzantines, it went on to become a stable possession of the Lombards up until its inclusion in the Marches of Tuscany (11C). It became an independent free commune in the 12C. With the setting up of the Captaincy of the People (i.e. controlled by the "condottiere" - a leader of troops) (mid 13C), Orvieto enjoyed a period of prolific artistic and political advancement, extending its possessions from the coastal regions of the Maremma (Orbetello) to the region of Mt Amiata and the valley of the Tiber. From the 13C, Orvieto was the scene of the fatal battles fought between the local "bigwigs" i.e. the Guelph faction (Monaldeschi) and the Ghibellines (Filippeschi). It was annexed by Cardinal Albornoz to the Papal State (second half of the 14C) and then conquered by Rinaldo Orsini, Biordo Michelotti., Braccio Fortebraccio and by the Monaldeschi della Vipera nobles. Later it became a favourite refuge of the popes, due to its easily defensible strategic position (a well-known feature of the town being St Patrick's well, near the fortress, built on the orders of Pope Clement VII in the first half of the 16C). At this time Orvieto enjoyed a flourishing artistic and cultural period, thanks to the patronage of prelates and the local aristocracy. Under Napoleon Bonaparte, Orvieto became an important administrative centre up until its re-establishment (1816). It was annexed to the newly formed Kingdom of Italy by an army of volunteer troops united under the insignia of the Cacciatori del Tevere (Huntsmen of the Tiber) (1860). Today, Orvieto is one of the most beautiful towns in Italy, and tourists flock here in their thousands, drawn by the rich array of Urban medieval features and the shining architectural characteristics, which repre-*

97

Orvieto, the splendid decorative Gothic façade of the Cathedral

sent a kind of continuity between the Gothic and Renaissance styles. The vast proportions of its cultural, artistic and monumental heritage are complemented by the delicious specialities of the local cuisine, accompanied by the Orvieto Bianco - the indisputable "prince" of Umbrian wines. The olive groves situated around the district produce an excellent quality of olive oil. The composite handicraft industry features the production of ceramics (artistic paving and wall tiles, jugs, vases etc), wrought ironware, jewellery, wood carving and manufacture, lace making and the manufacture of umbrellas. The most famous local festivities include the Festival of the "Palombella" *(horse race) (Whitsuntide), which has important analogies with the Florentine "Scoppio del Carro" (lit: Explosion of the Cart - a fireworks display)*, and the Procession of Corpus Domini, *with a pageant in historical costumes, to commemorate the miracle of Bolsena (1264).*

CATHEDRAL - The Cathedral was constructed on the site of the pre-existing cathedrals of St Mary and S.Costanzo in 1290. There are many doubts as to who designed the first construction (which was probably Romanesque). It is more widely attributed to Arnolfo di Cambio and Fra' Bevignate of Perugia. The first authentic references date back to 1308, when Lorenzo Maitani began restructuring work on some parts of the interior, the completion of the apse and the design and construction of the façade, which was completed in the first years of the 17C. After the death of the Siennese architect, the project was taken over by his son Vitale, Niccolò and Meo Nuti, Andrea and Nino Pisano, Matteo di Ugolino da Bologna, Andrea di Cecco da Siena and Andrea di Cione (Orcagna). Around the middle of the 15C, Antonio Federighi introduced some modifications inspired by Renaissance architecture, while in the 16C the construction work was supervised by several different architects, including Michele Sanmicheli, Giovanni Mosca, Moschino, Raffaello da Montelupo and Ippolito Scalza. Further work was carried out over the years, until the Cathedral of Orvieto was finally completed in the 17C, even if subsequent ornamental designs and restoration work have continued to be executed up until the present day. The **façade** is a stunning example of the decorative Gothic style, created by Lorenzo Maitani; it can be said to have reached completion in the first years of the 17C. The façade of the Cathedral rises up from a flight of dichromatic steps and is divided vertically by four enormous fluted pillars crowned with spires. In the lower part of the façade are three magnificent pointed portals. Above these is a charming small loggia, which separates the lower portion of the façade from the upper one. This series of small arches is crowned with spires and small aedicules and by three beautifully decorated triangular tympana. The centre of the façade contains Orcagna's masterly rose window., Due to the exquisite wealth of decorative sculptures and mosaics contained here, this section of the façade could almost be described as a separate "museum", even though several features have been restored or substituted by copies. The bas-reliefs visible in the lower portion of the façade depict *The Creation, the Prophecies of the Messiah, the Stories of the Gospel and The Last Judgement*. The bronze doors are contemporary works by Emilio Greco (1964). Above these, the bronze *Symbols of the Evangelists* are attributed to Maitani. The lunette above the main portal was once decorated by a 14C fresco depicting *Angels* and a 14C *Madonna in Judgement*, attributed to Arnolfo di Cambio (they have now been removed to a safer destination in order to undergo the usual interminable process of restoration). The figures of *Prophets* and *Apostles* which surround the rose window were executed between the 14C and the 16C (I.Scalza, F.Toti, R da Montelupo) The mosaic surrounding Orcagna's rose window is by Piero di Puccio (14C), who was also responsible for the mosaics which embellish the lateral triangular tympana. The highly

Orvieto, a side view of the Cathedral with its characteristic alternating black and white sections

Orvieto, lower section of the façade of the Cathedral: detail of the bas-reliefs

decorative **side walls** consist of alternating horizontal layers of black basalt and pale limestone. Also visible are the protruding apses of the side chapels and pointed portals (two on the left side, one on the right). The grandiose **interior** is divided into a nave and two aisles by robust central columns and pillars, which sustain the arches above. The interior is a mixture of Gothic and Renaissance styles. The christening font is the work of several different artists (Luca di Giovanni, Pietro di Giovanni, Iacopo di Pietro di Guido, Sano di Matteo, 14C-15C). The holy-water stoups are by A. Federighi, V. da Siena, I. Scalza, C. Cardinali. The apse, lit by 14C stained glass windows by Giovanni di Bonino, contains 14C frescoes by Ugolino di Prete Ilario, restored by Pinturicchio and by Pastura, and a wooden choir by G. Ammannati (14C). The side altars (*of the Visitation* and *of the Magi*) are by Moschino, Simone Mosca and Raffaello da Montelupo. In the right transept, behind an artistic wrought iron railing (16C), is the beautiful **Cappella Nuova** (New Chapel) (or

Orvieto, a view of the grandiose interior of the Cathedral

Chapel of *S.Brizio*). This chapel contains exquisite frescoes by Luca Signorelli and includes his superlative painting of the *Last Judgement*, considered to be one of the greatest frescoes in Italian Art. The chapel also contains medallions depicting poets and philosophers, ranging from Homer to Dante, with scenes from some of their works. This cycle of frescoes is considered to be one of the best examples of Renaissance art and is acclaimed as being the inspiration for Michelangelo's *Last Judgement* in the Sistine Chapel. Two of the ceiling vaults contain frescoes by Beato Angelico (*Prophets, Christ in Judgement*). On the 18C altar by B. Cametti is a painting depicting the *Madonna di S.Brizio* (13C). In the left transept stands the 14C **Cappella dei Corporale**, which one enters by means of a 14C wrought iron railing. The vaults and walls contain frescoes by Ugolino di Prete Ilario (14C). On the altar is the valuable *Tabernacle "del Corporale"*, by Nicolò da Siena and Orcagna, which contains the *reliquary "del Corporale"*, a silver casket by Ugolino di Vieri (14C). The reliquary contains the sacred "corporale" (altar cloth) of the Miracle of Bolsena (1263) and was the reason behind the institution of the feast of "Corpus Domini". Other features of the chapel include the 18C *Archangels* by A. Cornacchini and a *Madonna dei Raccomandati* by Lippi Memmi (14C). Finally, note should also be made of the 16C organ by Scalza, a wonderful 16C *Pieta*, again by Scalza, and the wooden pulpit by G. Mercanti (17C).

Orvieto, christening font in the interior of the Cathedral

SOLIANO PALACE - Also known as the *Palace of Bonifacio VIII*, the building dates back to the 13C. It is an imposing tufa construction and is characterized by an external flight of steps and pointed mullioned windows with three lights. Important museums are housed within the building. The ground floor rooms contain the **Museum of Emilio Greco**. The museum has only recently been set up and includes numerous sculptures, bronze bas-reliefs and interesting ink drawings, which give an insight into the artistic production of the sculptor from Catania. One of the outstanding features of the museum is a plaster altar-piece, a perfect copy of the *Monument to Pope John XXIII*, the original can be seen at the Vatican.

On the first floor is the **Cathedral Museum**. This contains paintings, detached frescoes and church furnishings. Artists whose works are on show include S. Martini, L. Signorelli, A., Pisano, U. di Vieri and V. di Lando. Nearby stands the *Buzi Palace* (16C), designed by Ippolito Scalza.

THE FAINA CIVIC AND ARCHAEOLOGICAL MUSEUM - The collections are housed in the **Faina Palace**, which stands opposite the Cathedral. The exhibits, donated by Count Claudio Faina to the municipality, include objects from the Greek period, but above all artefacts dating from Etruscan times (jewellery, bronzes and vases). One of the most outstanding Etruscan exhibits is a *Sarcophagus* decorated with reliefs and traces of designs (4C BC.).

THE POPES'PALACE - Formerly the residence of a long line of popes, the construction has three wings built in the second half of the 13C. Restored in the 1960s, it now houses the **Archaeological Museum**, which has collections of burial apparel, and objects found in the Etruscan necropolises in the surrounding district.

THE CHURCH OF ST FRANCIS - The church was built as part of a convent in the 13C, and reconstructed in the 18C. The **façade** still contains the three pointed portals and two small rose windows which belonged to the original building. The **interior**, which has one central nave, contains Baroque features. Worthy of note are the beautiful carved 18C choir and a wooden *Crucifix* by pupils of Maitani.

THE CHURCH OF S. LORENZO DE ARARI - The church is a 13C construction characterized by Romanesque architecture. It has a 15C portal and a beautiful bellcote. The basilica-like interior consists of one nave

Orvieto, a view of the Popes' Palace which houses the Archaeological Museum

Orvieto: the Church of St Andrew with its unusual twelve-sided bell tower and the Church of S. Giovenale with its robust bell tower

and two aisles. It contains an interesting high altar originating from an Etruscan altar, with a 12C aedicule. The walls of the church have 14C frescoes.

TOWN HALL - The building looks out over the central *Piazza della Repubblica*, which was probably the site of the centre of the Etruscan-Roman town (it is likely that the Roman Forum stood here). The present building is the result of reconstruction work carried out by Scalza in the second half of the 16C. The Church is Romanesque in origin (13C).

THE CHURCH OF ST ANDREW - This historical building, which played an important part in several episodes of the town's history, was built between the 6C and the 14C, on the site of a pre-existing Early Christian church. Its brick **façade** has a large splayed portal, surmounted by a rose window. The adjacent twelve-sided brick **bell tower** is a masterly architectural compliment to the church and has three orders of mullioned windows with two lights and a turreted top section. On the left side of the church stands a portico. The **interior** has one nave and two aisles and contains a raised transept with cross vaults. Worthy of note are a wooden altar by I. Scalza, a pulpit by the Cosmatesque sculptors and the funeral aedicule attributed to artists from the workshop of Arnolfo di Cambio. Below the church are ancient ruins, which date from the Iron Age to the medieval period.

THE CHURCH OF ST GIOVENALE - This place of worship, originally a Romanesque building, was rebuilt in the 13C and contains Lombard features. To the side of the simple, bare **façade** stands a massive **bell tower**. The interior has a nave and two aisles; worthy of note are the high altar decorated with reliefs, - an exquisite Romanesque work. The transept is in the Gothic style. The walls have frescoes containing votive motifs by the Orvieto school (13C-16C).

PORTA MAGGIORE (THE MAIN GATE) - It is the most ancient of all the town gates. The *Statue of Bonifacio VIII* was built to commemorate the peace established between the town and the pope. The statue is a modern work.

THE CHURCH OF ST JOHN - The Church has medieval origins (11C) and was rebuilt in the 16C. The adjoining building, formerly the Convent of the Laterans, contains a 16C **Cloister**.

PALACE OF THE SETTE NOBLES - Formerly the *Della Terza Palace*, it was a judicial seat and a Papal residence. The imposing **Moro Tower**, a square shaped 13C building is 42 metres in height.

GUALTERIO PALACE - A 16C construction, the result of reconstruction work carried out by S. Mosca. It is characterized by a fine portal built by Ippolito Scalza and an internal courtyard.

CLEMENTINI PALACE - Construction work on this building was begun by Antonio da Sangallo (15C-16C) and completed by Ippolito Scalza. The ground floor houses the **Town Library** which contains over 80,000 books.

THE TOWER OF MAURIZIO - The tower dominates the *Cathedral Square;* it was originally built as a sundial and is thought to be one of the most ancient clock towers in Italy. *Maurizio,* a small bronze statue, which strikes the hours, dates from the 14C. Nearby stands the **Netti Palace**, a Renaissance construction.

THE THEATRE - Dedicated to the musician Luigi Mancinelli, the theatre is a 19C construction designed by Vespignani and G Santini of Perugia. The frescoes in the interior are by C. Fracassini and Angelini.

CAPTAIN OF THE PEOPLE'S PALACE - An imposing 12C-13C turreted building, decorated by mullioned windows with three lights and ornamental moulding. On the ground floor is an external flight of steps leading up to a fine portal.

THE CURCH OF ST DOMENIC - The original church dates from the 13C; the present day building is the result of later alterations, which have reduced the size of the building. The Gothic portal visible in the **façade** was transferred here from another place of worship. St Thomas Acquinas taught in the *studium* of the Church (the desk at which he taught is still visible). One of the outstanding features of the **interior** is the 13C *Tomb of Cardinal de Bray* by Arnolfo di Cambio. There is also a wonderful wooden *Crucifix.* The **Petrucci Chapel**, situated under the apse, was built by Michele Sanmicheli.

ALBORNOZ FORTRESS - Ugolino di Montemarte is attributed as having built the fortress at the behest of Cardinal Egidio Albornoz (14C).

Orvieto, a view of the imposing bastions of the Albornoz Fortress

Orvieto, a view of the Fortress Gate and the inside of St Patrick's Well

Environs of Orvieto. The Abbey of SS. Severo and Martirio, a view of the abbey with its twelve-sided tower; the village of Prodo with the Castle of Prodenzani, built of local pink stone

Nearby stands the **Fortress Gate**, which was built during the same period as the fortress itself; it was later restored by Lorenzo Maitani.

ST PATRICK'S WELL - St Patrick's Well, and the Cathedral, are the most famous constructions in Orvieto. It was known as the *Fortress Well* in ancient times and was built on the instructions of Pope Clement VII. It was intended to serve as a reservoir providing water to the nearby fortress (built by Albornoz) in the event of the city being besieged. The ingenious design for this masterly piece of Renaissance architecture was the work of Antonio da Sangallo the Younger, who completed the project in the first half of the 16C. Around the cylindrical cavity, which has a depth of 61.32 metres, are two parallel concentric staircases (each one having 248 steps), which never cross (the stairs are lit by large windows). The water carriers and their donkeys used one of the spiral staircases for going up and another for going down, getting in and out of the well by different entrances. According to Vasari, Antonio da Sangallo drew inspiration for this project from the internal staircase of the bell tower of the Church of St.Nicholas in Pisa.

TEMPLE OF BELVEDERE - The few remaining ruins of a 5C BC. Etruscan construction are situated in the public gardens next to the Albornoz Fortress. Some ornamental details of the pediment are on display in the Faina Archaeological Museum.

ETRUSCAN NECROPOLISES - The necropolises were built at the bottom of a tufa formation, upon which the first Etruscan settlements were formed. The **Necropolis of the Tufa Crucifix** to the north and the **Necropolis of Cannicella** to the south east, date from the 6C BC. Interesting remains of chamber tombs and burial apparel have been discovered on this site.

ENVIRONS - The Premonstratensian **Abbey of SS. Severo and Martirio** (12C) is dominated by a superb twelve-sided brick tower, crowned with merlons. The structure of this Romanesque tower, commissioned by Matilde di Canossa at the beginning of the 12C, is decorated by mullioned windows with one and two lights. The church of the abbey contains masterly 13C-14C frescoes and a remarkable floor built by the Cosmatesque marble sculptors. **Sugano**, a charming village situated along the high green plateau of Alfina, looks down on the city of Orvieto, in an enchanting scenic location. It is an extremely ancient village, dating back to the first Etruscan settlements of the 4C BC. In medieval times, it became a fief of the Monaldeschi della Cervara nobles and was also a fortified outpost in the territory of Bolsena. The locality is renowned for the basalt quarry situated here, and enormous amounts of igneous rock were used to construct many of the buildings in the City of Orvieto. Here too are situated the underground springs containing the curative waters of the Tione; thriving wrought iron and Irish lace making handicraft industries are also situated at Sugano. The ancient village of **Prodo** is characterized by the imposing structure of the **Prodenzani Castle** (13C). A former possession of the Cathedral of Orvieto, the local pink stone used in its construction, make the castle one of the eye-catching features of the surrounding landscape. From the top of a rocky ledge, its towers keep vigil over the converging valleys situated towards the Tiber. **Titignano**, an outpost of the city of Orvieto, stands near the confines of the district of Todi. It was built as a medieval castle, becoming a noble residence between the 16C and 17C.

LAKE CORBARA - Lake Corbara, situated near Titignano, is a popular fishing spot. Furthermore, its close proximity to the impressive cavities known as the **Wells of the Plain** make it a well known tourist attraction.

OTRICOLI

The modern town stands on a ridge dominating the Valtiberina and the *Via Flaminia,* not far from the interesting archaeological zone of *Ocriculum.* An ancient Umbrian foundation, built between the 4C and 3C BC., it was an important centre in Roman times. Handicraft industries at Otricoli include the production of ceramics and porcelain objects; the *Wine Festival* and an exhibition of local produce are held in September. The excavations at **Ocriculum** have uncovered interesting archaeological finds, the majority of which date back to Roman times. The campaign undertaken by Pope Pius VI is particularly well known. In the Vatican Museums, it is possible to admire a considerable amount of archaeological exhibits, which were found in this particular corner of Umbria: the most well-known exhibits are the *Head of Jove of Otricoli* and the famous *Spa Mosaic*.

PACIANO

An ancient medieval village which has splendid panoramic views ranging from Trasimeno and its surrounding lowland district to the relict lakes of Chiusi and Montepulciano and the sweeping expanses of the Valdichiana. The present day village still has its medieval configuration, and parts of the ancient **town walls** with pointed gates and turreted towers can be seen. The ruins of a Franciscan convent and the so-called **Tower of Orlando** are the most outstanding features which remain of the ancient settlement. The **Town Hall**, together with the **Rastrella** and **Florentine** gates date back to the 14C. The **Perugia Gate** is an 18C construction. The **Church of St Joseph** contains a banner painted by a pupil of Bonfigli. The **Church of St Charles** has a fine 17C portal.
The ancient monastery of the **Brotherhood of the Sacrament** has been transformed into a picture gallery.

PENNA IN TEVERINA

An enchanting village situated on a ridge, dominating the confluence of the Tiber and the Rio Grande. References to the Castle of Penna were made in official deeds dating back to the 14C. Nowadays, Penna in Teverina is known for its delicious traditional cuisine, which is perfectly accompanied by the good quality local wines. In August the *Sagra del Tortiglione* is held, while in the month of October, the locality celebrates the *Wine Harvest Festival* and the *Festival lungo un giorno, lungo un anno* (lit. for a day, for a year) (Autumn). Ruins of a **Roman Villa** were discovered in **Penna Vecchia**. The importance of the building is underlined by the presence of a mosaic floor and a furnace. A Roman shipping port is believed to have been situated in this area. On either side of the **Civic Gate** are ancient stone benches. The characteristic small piazza of the village is dominated by the **Governor's Palace**. The **Orsini Palace** has the insignia of the Orsini and the Anguillara families. The palace grounds contain a beautiful 19C Italianate garden.

PIEGARO

A charming small town perched on a hill-top dominating the point at which the Diavolo stream flows into the Nestore river. The first inhabitants were most probably Umbrians and Etruscans, however unequivocal evidence has ascertained that the first settlements were established here by the Romans in 290 BC. This small town is famous for the manufacture of glass - in particular the production of flasks and demi-johns. Piegaro's glass-making traditions go back to the end of the 13C, when a community of craftsman from Murano settled here after an edict of the Serene Republic of Venice had imposed the closure of the ovens used in the process of glass making. The ancient medieval configuration of this small town is still discernible in stretches of the **town walls** and ruins of the fortifications. The **Parish Church** is dedicated to *St Sylvester*. A *Crucifix,* held in popular belief to be miraculous, is kept in its interior. Worth a mention in the surrounding district of Piegaro are the **Castle** and **Tower** of **Castiglione Fosco,** ruins of the ancient city of **Fallera** on the mountain bearing the same name, and the **Sanctuary of the Madonna delle Grondici.**

PIETRALUNGA

Pleasantly situated on a hill-top between the Carpina and Carpinella streams, the town was once an ancient centre founded by the Umbrians. It was also inhabited by the Romans from whose epoch remain the ruins of some villas and other archaeological finds which induce us to suppose that here, there once stood the *Forum Julii Concubiense*.

Among the specialities of the place, mention should be made of a particular strain of potato, whilst truffles and mushrooms are recommended, when in season. Wide stretches of the **town walls** and the ruins of a **Stronghold** erected by the Lombards (8C) are some of the interesting features to be found in the centre of **Pietralunga. The Sanctuary of the Madonna dei Rimedi** is a charming stone construction with an annexed bell tower and a small portico on the façade. The **Parish Church of Pietralunga** contains a fresco depicting the *Martyrdom of St Sebastian*, attributed to Raffaellino del Colle. Sports and leisure fans can take full advantage of the facilities on offer at the tourist complex of **Candeleto,** set in a splendid scenic location.

The **Parish Church of the Saddi,** not far from Pietralunga, is worth a mention. This country church is believed to have been built over a pagan temple.

POLINO

The village is situated on top of a ridge, a short distance from the Lazio border, in a valley of the lower Valnerina. Its pleasant setting on the far north-western spurs of the Reatini mountains and the decidedly medieval air of the ancient settlement, makes it one of those minor centres in Umbria which nonetheless deserve a mention. Its foundation dates from the Middle Ages, and over the centuries, due to the presence of marble quarries, iron deposits and a silver mine, it was an important mining centre. Today the economy of the area is based essentially on the primary sector, even though many of the inhabitants commute to Terni. Old stone houses and narrow paved alleyways can still be seen in the ancient nucleus, while a polygonal **Tower,**and the ruins of ancient fortifications dominate the medieval village. The nearby zone of **Monte La Pelosa** (1635m) has recently been developed as both a summer and winter resort, and has modern skiing facilities.

Polino, a view of the medieval village situated amongst the green Umbrian hills

SAN GEMINI

A well-known town in the district of Terni, it is situated in gentle, hilly countryside, close to the Martani Mountains. San Gemini is divided into two distinct sections, consisting of an ancient medieval village and a more recently-developed area which spreads out along the main road leading to the Spa proper. The town grew in importance during the Middle Ages in an area which was once inhabited by the Romans (as can be proved by the nearby archaeological remains of *Carsulae*). Control of San Gemini was then granted to the popes by Henry II of Bavaria. Subsequently, it came under the rule of Narni and Todi and subdued by the Orsini family who made it into a Duchy in the final decade of the 16C. It received the title of city from Pope Pius VI in 1781. Its fortunes as a spa go back to the 19C, when systematic studies of the curative properties of the waters were undertaken. The best-known festival, which takes place in September and October, is the *Giostra dell'Arme,* which is the historical commemoration of a medieval competition.

Interesting buildings and features of the medieval centre include: the **Palazzo del Popolo** (People's Palace) characterized by a tower, (which has been reduced in height), and an external flight of steps; the one-naved **Church of St Francis** (13C to 14C) with its characteristic Gothic architecture, and the **Church of St John** with, on the left side, the ancient Romanesque façade enhanced with a portal bearing mosaic decorations of the Cosmatesque school. A short way from the centre is the beautiful Romanesque **Church of St Nicholas.** Its stone façade contains a central oculus and is adorned with a fine portal and a flight of steps decorated with historical scenes and lions bearing columns. At its side rises a delightful stone bell gable. The **San Gemini Spa** is situated at **San Gemini Fonte.** The cold *Sangemini* and *Fabia* waters have a calcium- bicarbonate content and are used to treat digestive problems, metabollic and liver disorders, urinary infections, as well as disorders of the biliary tract.

CARSULAE - The archaeological area of Carsulae is laid out in glorious surroundings in the green heart of the Umbrian countryside. The ancient Roman city, dates back to the 3C BC and was abandoned following a disastrous earthquake. Of outstanding interest are a stretch of the consular road, the Spa complex**,** the **Amphitheatre**, the **Theatre** and the **Trajan Arch (**or of *St Damian).* Nearby stands the small early-medieval church of **St Damian.**

San Gemini, a view of the ancient centre lying in the heart of typical Umbrian countryside

Carsulae (San Gemini), the Trajan Arch (also known as the Arch of St Damian)

SAN GIUSTINO

Situated in the upper Valtiberina, practically on the borders with Tuscany, San Giustino is the chief town of a territory which is interesting for its historical content, ancient ruins and architectonic elements. Many important road networks intersect here and it is situated at the beginning of the road leading to the Bocca Trabaria and stretches out along important roads of access connecting Umbria with Tuscany and Romagna. It was founded by the Umbrians - as various findings have ascertained. Populated during Roman times (it takes its name from the Christian martyr), it was subdued in the Middle Ages to various families (Dotti and then Bufalini), finally passing under the control of Città di Castello. The history of the town was determined by the fortunes of Cospaia, a tiny village which set itself up as an autonomous republic for 386 years between the fifteenth and nineteenth centuries, thereby taking advantage of the struggles between the Tuscan and Papal governors and becoming a thriving centre as a result of money gained through tobacco smuggling.

Noted for its lace, ceramics and for antique and reproduction furniture, San Giustino is also famous for the exquisite truffles which can be tasted here, washed down with the excellent Panicale wine. Outstanding among the folk festivals is the Corpus Domini Flower Festival, the *Infiorata* which originated in the 17C.

The stately 15C **Bufalini Castle** looks like a mighty fort encircled by great imposing corner towers and crowned with a bell tower. However, the refined elegance of Vasari's loggia and the wide profusion of decorations in the interior (frescoes by Cristoforo Gherardi, known as "Doceno", Signorelli and Guido Reni; antique furnishings; Roman busts from a villa which probably belonged to Pliny the Younger), show that it was later converted into a leisure haunt and princely residence. The castle is surrounded by a green park with Italianate gardens.

In the **Church of S. Andrea a Selci** a precious *Enthroned Madonna and Saints,* by Francesco da Castello (16C) can be seen.

In the district of **Colle Plinio**, excavations of a **Roman Villa**, believed to have belonged to Pliny the Younger, can be admired. Not far off, at **Celalba**, stands the splendid **Villa Margherini-Graziani**, the result of a 17C transformation of an ancient manor house. Of note is the interesting turretted crowning.

SCHEGGIA AND PASCELUPO

The small, widespread villages which make up the commune of Sheggia and Pascelupo are located in the upper valley of the Sentino river, in an area characterized by the mountainous slopes of Mt Cucco. During the decline of the Roman Empire, Scheggia was an important location along the communication routes situated north of the Apennines, especially the stretch of road between Rome and Ravenna. The *Statio ad Ensem* was once situated along the Via Flaminia. Among these mountains there once stood a temple consecrated to Jove of the Apennines; the famous Eugubine tablets (together with a wealth of other archaeological finds) were discovered in this region. These were later moved to the city of Gubbio. The **Parish Church of St Philip and St James** is the result of re-construction work (late 18C) carried out on a pre-existing place of worship, which collapsed after an earthquake. Of the original six towers which defended this important intersection, only one medieval **Tower** remains standing. The **Parish Church of S. Paterniano** has been converted into a private residence. The **Abbey of S. Maria di Sitria** (12C) is situated at the foot of Mount Catria. Of note is the external facing in calcareous stone. The interior has a Latin cross plan and one single nave.
The **Hermitage of S. Emiliano in Congiuntoli** (11C) was founded by St Romuald. The Gothic church has two naves. The 17C **Sanctuary of Monte Calvario** is situated on the hill dominating Scheggia. In its interior is a precious wooden *Crucifix* dating back to the 16C.
The whole district offers visitors interesting excursions in the beautiful natural surroundings of the Umbrian-Marches Apennines (Monte Catria and Monte Cucco).

SELLANO

A charming village near the Marches border, it stands on a hillock surrounded by wooded rises. It was probably founded by the followers of Silla in 84 BC. In this district (village of Villamagina), the age-old production of files and rasps by local craftsmen is still a thriving activity. The gastronomical traditions of the area are revived during the *Village Festival of the Wild Boar and the Truffle* (August) and the *Thanksgiving and Country Festival* (October). The **Town Hall** has a 16C façade and contains 16C fragmentary frescoes in its interior. The fresco attributed to Paolo da Visso dates from the mid 15C. The **Church of St Francis** dates from the first half of the 16C. A building with an octagonal plan, it is preceded by a pronaos with tympanum; on the inside there is a chapel with 16C altars. The 13C **Church of St Mary** is the fruit of reconstruction work carried out in the 16C. In the interior is a carved walnut pulpit, a triptych with a gold background (15C) and paintings dating back to the 16C and 17C.

SIGILLO

The village of Sigillo stretches out on both sides of the Via Flaminia, along the stretch of foothills dominated by the summit of Mt Cucco (1566 m). Here, there once stood the ancient Roman *Municipium* of *Suillim*, which played a fundamental role in the regulation and supervision of trading along the consular road. The surrounding countryside was the scene of the battle between the troops of Totila and Narsete (552). Later, it became an important centre along the so-called "Byzantine corridor" which facilitated trading between Rome and Ravenna. Subsequently it underwent periods of strife and upheaval and was even destroyed by Frederick II (1230). After having been rebuilt by Perugia, a long period of its history was then inextricably bound to the city's own destiny. However, although it benefited from Perugia's protection, it was also subjected to heavy taxation.
The hang-gliding school known as the "Centro di volo libero Monte Cucco" is situated at Sigillo. A feast day to be remembered is that of *S. Anna* (26 July). The **Town Hall** dates from the 12C, although its Neo-classical façade dates from the 19C. The Church of **S. Maria di Scirca** is a beautiful 13C place of worship. The interior has commendable frescoes by Matteo da Gualdo portraying the *Madonna della Misericordia*, an

Enthroned Virgin and *S. Anna.* The **Church of St Augustine** (second half of the 18C) was built over the ancient Crypt of St Catherine. In the interior is a 17C painting (*Annunciation*). Although references to the **Church of St Andrew** date back as far as the 13C, the present church was reconstructed between the 17C and 19C. The **Church of Sant'Anna al Cimitero** (15C) contains a masterly cycle of frescoes by Matteo da Gualdo. An exceptional example of Augustan architecture (even though some maintain that it is from the 3C BC), the **Spiano Bridge** stands a short distance from the village. Another bridge, called the **Dei Pietroni**, was blown up by the German troops in the last war. It was long held that these ruins were from the Etruscan period: however, nowadays it is more commonly believed that they date back to the Imperial age (2nd cent. AD).

SPELLO

A charming ancient town pleasantly situated on the southern slopes of Monte Subasio. In urban, architectural and artistic terms, Spello is an extremely interesting town, containing many features dating back to the Roman age and a medieval nucleus which has remained intact with Renaissance buildings blending in admirably. It was founded in the age of the Umbrians, became a flourishing Augustan colony (*Julia*), and was called *Flavia Constans* at the time of Constantine. The Barbarian invasions brought about the steady decline of the town, up until it came under the control of the Dukes of Spoleto. Subsequently it received a free, municipal constitution. However, it was then destroyed by Frederick 11. Afterwards, it was taken over by the Church and then fell to Perugia. Finally, it became part of the Papal states in 1583.
Weaving is still practised in the town. Among the local festivities, it is worth mentioning the *Festa dell'Olivo* (along with the village festival of bruschetta - toasted bread with oil and garlic - in February) and the *Flower Festival of Corpus Domini.*

Spello, the characteristic flower carpets of Corpus Domini

*Spello, a view of the Consular Gate with statues dating back
to the Republican period*

The historical centre of Spello is still by and large included within the
circle of its ancient **walls;** ample stretches of these walls, as well as
some of the major entrance gates date back to Roman times.
The **Consular Gate** dates back to the time of Augustus. It is a noteworthy example of a Roman gate with three arches. In the upper portion
three statues dating back to the Republican period can be seen.
Unequivocal evidence has proved that these were transferred from the
archaeological area to this site. This gate, which nowadays has one wide
central opening (the side arches have sunk down into the ground) is the
main entrance to the town. Today (as in Roman times) it lies directly
along a side-street which connects it with the Via Flaminia. To the side
of the gate (whose structure and features resemble those of another famous town gate - the Gate of Venus) stands a robust tower, built during
medieval reconstruction work on the walls and surrounding areas.
Beyond the gate, stands the medieval district known as Borgo, which is
characterized by the warm tones of Subasio stone, its paved streets and
the rustic stone and brick façades of its medieval houses.
The 14C **Tega Chapel** has interesting frescoes by 15C Umbrian artists.
Other outstanding works include a *Crucifixion* by Alunno and a *Maestà*
by Pietro di Mazzaforte.
The **Church of S. Maria Maggiore** has ancient origins (11C), even
though restoration work was carried out in the second half of the 13C.
Around the mid 17C, this place of worship, built over the remains of an
altar consecrated to Juno and Vesta, was profoundly transformed. The

Romanesque portal (13C) is a noteworthy work by the marble-workers Binello and Rodolfo. In the Baroque interior, is the famous Baglioni Chapel, containing frescoes executed in 1501 by Pinturicchio (Bernardino di Betto), portraying the *Annunciation*, the *Dispute in the Temple*, the *Nativity* and the *Sibyls*. The floor consists of valuable Deruta majolica tiles (16C). In the small museum next door, paintings from the period between the 14C and 16C can be admired.

The **Church of St Andrew** has a 13C façade, whereas the interior (which has been subjected to several transformations over the years) contains frescoes of the Foligno school (15C). Noteworthy features include the large canvas by Pinturicchio depicting the *Virgin and Child Enthroned with Saints*, and a *Crucifix* executed in the style of Giotto.

The imposing **Gate of Venus** is enclosed between the twin twelve-sided **Propertius Towers**. This mighty construction with three supporting arches is a superlative example of Roman architecture.

The **Ancient Town Hall** is the work of Maestro Prode, according to an epigraph on the façade. The building still retains a few parts of the original 13C construction. Note the 16C fountain and the atrium, with a dis-

Spello, the Church of S. Maria Maggiore

115

play of archaeological finds. A **Museum-Picture Gallery** has been set up in the palace. Amongst the numerous exhibits on show, many archaeological finds discovered in the area near the amphitheatre can be admired (ornamental decorations, stone objects). One of the museum's most interesting exhibits is the so-called *rescript of Constantine*, an edict in which laws granting special privileges to the town are set out. Near the Town Hall there once stood a *Fortress*. Of this building, which was constructed in the second half of the 14C, and was probably the residence of the rector of the Duchy of Spoleto, no visible remains can be seen except for an epigraph in the atrium of the Town Hall.

The **Church of St Laurence** was built in the 12C, even though successive transformations carried out between the 16C to 17C are clearly visible. In the 17C interior, is the Chapel of the Sacrament, inside which is a late 16C marble tabernacle, by Flaminio Vacca. The wooden choir bears engravings from the 16C. The 17C wooden crib should also be noted.

Through the **Arch of Augustus**, which dates from the Augustan age, one comes to the **Church of S. Maria di Vallegloria**, with an adjoining monastery (containing a fine **Cloister** dating from the second half of the 16C). The building, which dates from the first half of the 14C, houses 16C and 17C frescoes.

The **Church of St.Jerome,** with its adjoining Convent, dates back to the 15C. In front of the building, there is a Renaissance-style portico frescoed by 15C Umbrian painters. A small chapel preserves frescoes by pupils from the workshop of Pinturicchio. The interior contains a wooden *Crucifix* (16C) and a fresco painted in the style of the pupils of Pinturicchio.

The **Town Gate,** or *Gate of S. Ventura*, has one single entrance-way and dates back to the Augustan age. Decorated with a triangular tympanum, it is inserted into a stretch of the Roman and medieval walls. Not to be forgotten is the small, but charming **Church of St Martin** (Romanesque) and the **Porta dell'Arce** (or *Capuchin Arch*), an ancient Roman construction, situated in a panoramic spot overlooking the Valle Umbra. Near the gate, which is also known as the *Roman Arch* stands the convent of the Capuchin friars and the **Church of S. Severino**. The façade of the original Romanesque church is connected to the apse of the present day building. At the highest point of the town, on the summit of a lovely hill covered with cypress trees stand a few large towers. These are all that remain of a medieval Fortress which was probably constructed by Albornoz (14C). Unequivocal evidence has shown that defence fortifications were built on the higher parts of Spello as far back as ancient times. As well as the afore-mentioned Roman Arch (or *Capuchin Arch*, also known as *Porta dell'Arce*), ruins of a Roman construction can be seen near a privately owned house. Later, the Lombards set up their military encampment on this spot. In the Early Middle Ages, several houses were built around a 6C parish church (the original church of S. Severino). Subsequently, when the settlements along the plain and outside the town walls were abandoned because of their vulnerable position, this settlement grew into a hill village (above all from the period of the free communes onwards).

Outside the walls, stand the ruins of the **Roman Amphitheatre** (1C AD). Today, only fragments of flooring, pilasters and other ruins remain of this construction which must once have been a considerably important feature of the ancient town.

Nearby stands the beautiful Romanesque façade of the **Church of S. Claudius** (12C). Constructed in Assisi stone, it is decorated by a mullioned window with two lights and a lovely rose window. On the roof of the church is an interesting double-ordered bell gable. Numerous frescoes from the Umbrian school are housed in the interior. Those above the apse, believed to have been painted by Cola Petruccioli, (14C) are outstanding.

The 16C Villa Fidelia, was transformed in the eighteenth and nineteenth centuries and has a delightful Italianate garden. The *Straka-Coppa Collection* (pictures, sculptures and antiques) is on show inside the villa.

The **Tonda Church** was built in the first half of the 16C by architects of the Lombard school. The church has a Greek-cross plan and is domianted by an octagonal-shaped dome. It has a superlative 16C portal, believed to be the work of Simone Mosca. The interior is decorated with numerous frescoes of the Umbrian school, including one by Mezzastris (1533).

Spoleto, a panoramic view of the town centre

SPOLETO

HISTORICAL BACKGROUND - *The city is situated on a sunny hillside, surrounded by green rises, at the lower border of the Valle Umbra, near the Tessino river which flows alongside the most recently-developed town districts. A centre founded by the Umbrians, with probably Etruscan influences, it was Romanized at the time of the Samnite Wars. It was a colony under Latin law (Spoletium, 241 BC) and was a faithful ally of Rome in the latter's struggle against the Carthaginians. During the course of the second Punic War, it withstood the onslaught of Hannibal's armies, thereby impeding the Carthaginian general to continue his advance on Rome. Having become a* Municipium, *it suffered the consequences of the Civil War and was sacked in 80 BC. After the fall of the Roman Empire, Spoleto was the capital of a flourishing Lombard duchy. Round about the mid 12C, it was destroyed by Frederick I and was subjected to severe damage shortly afterwards at the hands of the archbishop Cristiano di Magonza. Having become one of the Papal possessions, it became a favourite residence of the popes. However it was later to become one of the many Umbrian towns in which the battles between the Guelph and the Ghibelline factions were fought out. As a result, it was then was subdued by Perugia. Having been liberated by Albornoz, it subsequently came under the Visconti family, Braccio da Montone and Pirro Tomacelli. In the second half of the 14C, it rose up, together with Todi, against the excessive power of the popes, but it was taken over by Giuliano della Rovere and entrusted to Lucrezia Borgia. In 1809 it became the main town of the French Department of Trasimeno and was annexed to the newly-formed State of Italy on 17 September 1860.*
The present-day urban lay-out of Spoleto is particularly interesting (above all in the ancient town centre which is still, for the most part, surrounded by ancient town walls). Furthermore, its archaeological and artistic features make it one of the most popular attractions of Umbria. Traditional cultural events have long been part of the town's heritage and it also has many interesting handcraft industries (cloth, lace and embroidery, horse saddles and harnesses, model-making equipment). The excellent cuisine, based on truffles and other local specialities, such as "strangozzi" (home-made pasta) provide even further attractions for tourists and sightseers. Among the most traditional festivities, mention should be made of the Carnival of Spoleto *(February and March); the* Week-long Seminar on the Early Middle Ages *(the week following Easter); the* Festival of the Two Worlds *(June and July);* the Opera Season of the Lyrical Experimental Theatre *(September); and the* Laud of the Nativity and the Living Crib *(24-25-26 December, 1 January).*

117

Spoleto, a splendid view of the Cathedral and its bell tower which is crowned by a spire

Spoleto, detail of the upper section of the façade of the Cathedral

CATHEDRAL - The Cathedral looks onto the **Piazza Duomo**, which is characterized by the 16C **Arroni Palace** (the decorations embellishing the façade are by Giulio Romano), the 16C **Church of S. Maria della Manna d'Oro,** the **Melisso Theatre** and by the building which houses the **Civic Museum.** The Cathedral is a Romanesque construction (12C), although its interior was transformed in the 17C. It has an impressive **façade,** preceded by a portico which was constructed between the 15C and 16C centuries. The façade, which was probably raised after the end of the 12C is embellished with five rose windows, the central one being surrounded by *Symbols of the Evangelists.* At the centre of the upper order, there is a precious mosaic executed by Solsterno and dated 1207, above which are situated three smaller rose windows. Beside the façade stands the imposing **Bell Tower** crowned with a spire. The tower is built from stones removed from former, ancient Roman constructions. The late Renaissance **interior**, has a plain, simple architectural configuration and is divided into a nave and two aisles. The nave still contains the original Romanesque flooring, with a large profusion of polychrome stone tesserae. On the counter - façade there is a *Bust of Urban VIII*, a masterly bronze work by Bernini. In the right aisle stands the **Chapel of Bishop Eroli,** frescoed by Pinturicchio, who depicted the *Pietà*, the *Eternal*, and the *Madonna with Child and Saints.* In the right portion of the transept is the *Sepulchral Monument of Fra' Filippo Lippi*, undertaken by his son, Filippino, with an epigraph by Poliziano. There is a painting of the *Virgin and Child with St Francis and St Dorothea*, by Annibale Carracci, at the altar (right transept). The apse glows with the magnificent frescoes executed by Filippo Lippi and his pupils (1467-69) on the themes of the *Annunciation*, the *Passing Away of the Virgin*, the *Nativity* and the *Coronation of the Madonna.* The **Reliquary Chapel** used to house a beautiful *Cross* painted by Alberto Sozio (1187), now situated to the left of the main entrance, and wooden sculptures by 16C Spoleto artists.

CHURCH OF S. EUFEMIA - A basilica-like building which is situated within the confines of the Bishopric, it is considered one of the finest examples of Umbrian-Romanesque architecture, even though the influence of Lombard architecture is much in evidence. Constructed in the first half of the 12C, its simple, bare **façade** is decorated by a portal, a window with one opening, a mullioned window with two lights and a series of arches on the crowning part. The austere and stark **interior**, is divided into three parts and has evident Lombard features in the women's gallery. These features are the only example of this style of architecture in the region. On the vault and on two columns on the right of the church, frescoes from the Umbrian school (15C) can be seen. An interesting feature is also the Cosmatesque altar-facing on the main altar (13C).

Spoleto, detail of the so-called Arch of Drusus

TOWN HALL - Built in the 13C, with only the tower remaining of the original building, it was substantially transformed in the 18C. The **Art Gallery** is housed here, and contains collections of detached frescoes, tapestries and various art exhibitions. Among the artists whose works are on show here, mention should be made of the Maestro of Cesi, Antonello da Saliba, Alunno, Spagna, S. Conca and Guercino.

ROMAN HOUSE -Interesting remains of a Roman dwelling dating back to the 1C AD are situated in *Via di Visiale,* directly underneath the west wing of the Town Hall. An epigraph, found during archaeological digs, bears a dedication which leads one to suppose that the house belonged to Vespasia Polla, the mother of Vespasiano. Two rooms are situated around a quadrangular atrium, complete with *Impluvium* and underlying cistern. Of interest are the remains of the *Tablinum* and *Triclinium,* (with fragments of ancient decorations), and the ruins of the *Peristilio* (with column bases), mosaics, household objects and ornamental decorations.

ARCH OF DRUSUS THE YOUNGER - It is situated near the so-called **Arch of Monterone** (probably a gate dating back to the 3C BC). The construction, which is also dedicated to *Germanicus* (the son of Drusus the Elder, and brother of Augustus) dates from the 1C AD and has one entrance-way, decorated with pilaster strips and Corinthian capitals. Nearby, a **Roman Temple**, part of the ancient Forum, has been brought to light. Around the temple, of which only a few remaining elements are visible, an Early-Christian church was constructed, which was later modified and built on another spot. The place of worship, today dedicated to *S. Ansano*, betrays 17C reconstruction work and contains a beautiful fresco by Spagna. Through the church, access is gained to the **Crypt of St Isaac** (12C), which has three small aisles, and 12C groin vaulting and frescoes. The nearby *Piazza del Mercato (Market Square)* has a walled- **Fountain** designed by Costantino Fiaschetti (18C), built on the site of the ancient Church of S. Donato. The four coats of arms, decorating the upper part of the fountain date back to the 17C. The designs are by Maderno, in honour of Urban VIII.

ROMAN THEATRE - A fine overall view of this 1C construction (AD) can be had from the overhanging *Piazza della Libertà*, near an arcaded façade, previously part of the 17C **Palazzo Ancaiani** stables. The semi-circle of the auditorium is well visible, whilst the medieval monastery of

St Agatha now stands on the site where the stage area used to be. However, the marble floor of the orchestra, which is quite well preserved, can still be admired.

CHURCH OF ST PHILIP - The façade of this building stands at the top of a wide sweep of steps. Despite the fact that it is a 17C construction, built during the Baroque period, the façade itself has simple, linear features. The building was designed by the architect Loreto Scelli, a native of the area. The **interior** has a Latin cross plan, with a nave and two aisles. and contains frescoes by G. Lapis, S. Conca and L. Baldi.

CHURCH OF ST JOHN AND ST PAUL - A simple stone construction built in the Romanesque period, the church dates back to the 12C. In the **interior,** valuable paintings, probably by a local 12C school of painting, can be admired. In particular, note in the presbytery *The Martyrdom of St John and St.Paul* and, on the left side, *The Martyrdom of St Thomas à Becket*, attributed to Alberto Sozio.

CHURCH OF ST NICHOLAS - The 14C building, with the annexed **Convent** is part of a vaster monumental complex, which also includes the **Church of S. Maria della Misericordia**. The **façade** is decorated with a fine Gothic portal; the one-naved **interior** is characterized by the raised apse.

NEW THEATRE - Most of the city's important cultural events are staged in this building which was constructed in the mid 19C. The **façade** is decorated with stuccos and medallions. Among the cultural institutions of Spoleto, mention must also be made of the 19C **Teatro Caio Melisso**, restored and reopened in Piazza del Duomo in 1958.

GALLERY OF MODERN ART - This is housed in the **Rosari Spada Palace**; the gallery contains works by distinguished artists who have made a mark on Italian art since the War. Among the numerous maestri of art represented here, are Elisa Montessori, Gianni Dessì, Alberto Burri, Ettore Colla, Pietro Consagra, Renato Guttuso, Arnaldo Pomodoro, Pompilio Mandelli, Giuseppe De Gregorio, Leoncillo Leonardi, Romano Notari and Domenico Gnoli.

Spoleto, a view of the Roman Theatre

Spoleto, the ancient Ponte dei Torri (Tower Bridge) which was originally an aqueduct

CHURCH OF ST DOMENIC - This 13C construction is characterized by its red and white fasciae and for its understated traits of Gothic architecture. On the right side, is situated an admirable Gothic portal. The grandeur of the bell tower is accentuated by a 16C loggia situated at the top. The **interior**, has one nave and an Egyptian cross plan and houses fine works of art, which include frescoes of the Umbrian school (15C), a 14C *Crucifix* and a large altarpiece by G. Lanfranco (*Virgin and Child with Saints*). The stupendous **St Mary Magdalene Chapel** is remarkable, as it is completely covered by frescoes depicting the *Life of the Saint.*

CITY WALLS - A very well-preserved stretch of the imposing city walls is visible in *Via Cecili*. The polygonal walls of the first stratum date back to the 6C BC and could be part of the defence system of the first Umbrian settlement. A double superimposition dating from the Roman period (IIIC - I BC) can also be seen.

RUINS OF THE ROMAN AMPHITHEATRE - The ruins of this grandiose 2C AD construction, are situated inside the Minervio Barracks. A vast raised piazza is all that remains of most of the auditorium and arena, whereas about ten arcades have been preserved. In the Middle Ages, the church of S. Gregorio Minore and other constructions stood on the site of the amphitheatre: the vaults of the ambulatories were turned into shops and the stones of the entire complex were used by Albornoz to build his fortress.

CHURCH OF ST GREGORY THE GREAT - Its construction goes back to the 12C. In front of the façade, there is a 16C portico which also forms part of the **Innocents' Chapel** (today the quadrangular-shaped Baptistery), the result of transformations carried out in the second half of the 14C. Note the ancient statues of *St Gregory* and *S. Parattale*, placed in two side niches. The imposing **Bell Tower** is contemporary to the foundation of the church. The interior, divided into a nave and two aisles, retains its original Romanesque character and contains a raised presbytery. A painting by S. Conca depicting *St Joseph* is kept here. The **Crypt,** which has five aisles, is worthy of note.

ROMAN BRIDGE - Ruins of this sunken bridge, dating back to the 1C AD, came to light in the 19C. Access to these ancient remains, situated under road level, is by means of steps which lead underneath the *Piazza della Vittoria*. The bridge, which at the time of construction joined the banks of the Tessino, is also called *Sanguinario* because it was situated near the amphitheatre, where the Christian martyrs were massacred.

VILLA REDENTA - Notable example of a noble residence dating back to the first years of the 19C. The villa is surrounded by a magnificent park which is open to the public.

CHURCH OF S. PONZIANO - This Romanesque place of worship is dedicated to the patron saint who, having been martyred, was buried where the church now stands. The two-ordered **façade** is crowned by a tympanum, the result of a later addition. Note the delightful portal, decorated

Environs of Spoleto: the Church of St Peter with its beautifully decorated façade

with cosmatesque reliefs, and the lovely, elaborate rose window. The **interior** is the result of a series of late 18C reconstructions. The **Crypt**, with a nave, two aisles and five apses, contains 14C and 15C votive frescoes.

BASILICA OF THE HOLY SAVIOUR - This ancient Early-Christian church was built, in all probability, in the 4C. The numerous transformations which ensued over the centuries have, moreover, altered the original configuration. One of the most outstanding parts of the **interior** is the presbytery, which is bathed in light and contains fine architectural detail, ornamental motifs and imposing Corinthian columns.

PONTE DELLE TORRI (lit. Tower Bridge) - The bridge, (which was originally an aqueduct) was probably built over a previous Roman construction, and was completed at the turn of the 13C. It is characterized by mighty piers (access is possible to the interior of two of these), and by high, narrow arcades.

FORTRESS - The towered mass of this stronghold dominates, with its mighty glacises, the view over Spoleto. Gattapone was commissioned by Albornoz to construct it, and he carried out the work in the second half of the 14C. The fortress, previously used as a prison, has an ample **Arms Courtyard** and the notable **Courtyard of Honour**.

CHURCH OF S. PAOLO INTER VINEAS - A 13C place of worship, which,in all probability, has even more ancient origins. Numerous reconstructions have been carried out over the years, particularly in the 18C. The 18C superstructures were, moreover, eliminated in 1966. The lovely Romanesque **façade** is characterized by a portal and a rose window. The **interior,** divided into a nave and two aisles, preserves fragmentary 13C frescoes in the transept.

ENVIRONS - The **Church of St Peter** stands out from the natural backdrop of Monteluco. The building, which dates from the 12C and 13C centuries, is preceded by a 17C sweep of steps. The beautiful **façade** is embellished with numerous ornamental decorations. The basilica-like **interior** has a nave and two aisles, as do the apses of the church. Interesting archaeolgical finds have been discovered in the area which lies opposite the church.
Worthwhile would be an excursion to nearby **Monteluco** (804m.), which used to be provide refuge for hermits. St Francis of Assisi founded a convent here, and this can still be seen today. The place has become a popular seasonal and holiday resort, and has a wealth of facilities situated in the environs of the uplands.
The ancient **Church of S. Giuliano (**12C), built on the site of a 6C church, has a **façade** which is mutilated in parts, with a mighty bell tower overhead. Remarkable are the portal and the ornamental decorations on the main façade, partially attributable to the Early-Christian period. The **interior,** divided into a nave and two aisles with semi-circular apses, has a raised presbytery and a Crypt.

STRONCONE

Stroncone lies near the Lazio border, in the fertile hills dominating the Terni basin, along the northern reaches of the Sabini Mountains. The town centre was founded in early medieval times (10C), and Stroncone was controlled by the abbots of Farfa and the Church State.
Interesting festivities are held here, the most outstanding of which are the *Good Friday Procession*, the *Corpus Domini Procession and Flower Festival*, the *Horse Market Fair* (June), the *National Vintage Car Rally* (July) and the *Sfida alla Berretta*, a historical commemoration of a medieval tournament (August).
In the town, where the remains of the medieval **town walls** and **towers** are visible, the **Church of St Francis** and the **Church of St John** stand out. The former was founded by the saint from Assisi in the first half of the 13C, and the latter is embellished with frescoes painted by the pupils of the Zuccari. There is a lovely, 17C **Fountain** in the square.
It is worth going on an excursion to **Prati**, a boundless high plain at 950m., recommended for summer holidays and weekend touring.

Terni, a view of the Cathedral and the portico situated in front of the façade

TERNI

HISTORICAL BACKGROUND - *In terms of size and population, Terni is the second largest city in Umbria (Perugia being the largest). It is the main town of the Province of Terni and spreads out over a large plain, along which the Tescino and Serra rivers run into that of the Nera. The first settlements in the area date back to the Bronze Age, although objects used in cremation ceremonies have been discovered in Villanovan localities and necropolises. It was probably a centre of Sabine foundation and, because of its geographical position, was known in ancient times as* Interamna Nahars, *or* Nahartium. *It constituted a flourishing* Municipium *under Rome but later fell into decline as a result of the incursions of the Barbarian populations. After its constitution as a free Commune, it was razed to the ground by Frederick I (1174) and endured various ups and downs, at times linked with the fortunes of the popes, at times with those of the emperors. From the first half of the 15C, it was included in the possessions administered by the Church. The city was developed in the modern age, when it finally managed to avoid being overcome by civil strife. During the second World War, Terni suffered considerable damage to its ancient urban structure on account of the numerous bombing raids.*

Today the city has a decidedly modern air about it, the outcome of post-War construction and an increase in building brought about by the growth of its industrial sector. Important iron, steel and metallurgical industries are to be found here, as well as many other local industries. In fact, Terni has one of the largest secondary sectors in Central Italy. Gold jewellery, costumes and masks are produced by the local handicraft industry. Piazza della Repubblica *is the fulcrum of civic activities and the popular meeting place of the city's inhabitants. Itinerant street markets (on Wednesdays and Saturdays) sell all types of merchandise, artisan products and flowers. Next*

125

Terni, the Spada Palace

to the market stalls is an unusual livestock market. As well as numerous concerts put on throughout the year, other important local festivals include the Exhibition of Gold Jewellery *(February) and the* Terni Cantamaggio *(the end of April)*

CATHEDRAL - The construction is the result of a 17C transformation of a Romanesque church. The ornate 12C main portal, is situated under a 17C portico which stands in front of the façade. The **interior,** divided into a nave and two aisles, contains a remarkable 16C wooden choir, a magnificent Baroque organ and a grandiose 18C tabernacle. Important paintings in the interior include an *Immaculate Conception*, executed by Flemish artists; a *Circumcision* and a *Presentation in the Temple* by Agresti (16C). Under the building an apsidal **Crypt**, divided into a nave and two aisles can be seen.

FAUSTO AMPHITHEATRE - The ruins of the amphitheatre (which date back to 32 AD) constitute some of the most tangible remains of the Roman presence in Terni. The building, which could accommodate up to 10,000 spectators, is situated near a stretch of the Roman **walls**.

CHURCH OF S. ALÒ - This small place of worship, with its graceful Romanesque features, was built around the year 1000, (although traces of reconstruction work are visible). One of its most interesting features is the external part of the apses. The **interior,** contains a painted **Cross** (13C) and 13C - 16C frescoes.

SPADA PALACE - Monumental Renaissance building, it is held to be the last project undertaken by Antonio da Sangallo the Younger, before he died in this Umbrian city in 1546. The stupendous stone **façade**, framed by a fine cornice, is flanked by two corner towers and has three large arches on the ground floor.

CHURCH OF THE HOLY SAVIOUR - An ancient and delightful construction, it is certainly the oldest church in Terni. The original building was a circular lantern (turret with windows all around) with arcades in the

Terni, the Church of the Holy Saviour: the façade

basement, and was constructed in the Early-Christian age (5C), probably built over a Roman house. The rectangular avant-corps is the result of a later, medieval addition (12C). The stark stone **façade** has a portal surmounted by a window with one opening and by a triangular gable with blind arches. The **interior** contains 13C fragmentary frescoes in the rotunda. Worthy of mention is the **Manassei Chapel**, the frescoes of which date back to the 14C.

PICTURE GALLERY AND ARCHAEOLOGICAL MUSEUM - These can be found in the **Manassei Palace** (17C). Paintings by illustrious artists, such as Gozzoli and Alunno, can be seen here, as well as a *Madonna* by the Master of the Annunciation Gardner, and paintings dated from between

Terni, the Church of the Holy Saviour: a view of the rotunda of the interior, which betrays its Early-Christian origins

the 16C and 18C (Federico Fiori and Antonio Gherardi). The archaeolgical collections include findings from various ages, brought to light in the surrounding areas.

CHURCH OF ST PETER - The church, with its annexed **Cloister** dates back to the 14C. The **façade** is embellished with a Gothic portal, decorated with a 15C relief(Christ blessing).
The aisleless **interior** has a vast polygonal apse and the 14C - 15C frescoes.

CHURCH OF ST LAURENCE - The building blends into the medieval quarter, which is characterized by the its ancient towers and houses. The church, which has 13C origins, underwent transformation work in the 17C. The **façade** is decorated with a portal (15C) and a mullioned window with three-lights. In the **interior**,which has two aisles, is a painting which dates from the end of the 16C depicting the *Martyrdom of St Blaise.*

CHURCH OF ST FRANCIS - Although the church was originally a 13C Gothic construction, the present day building is the result of 14C - 15C additions (Angelo da Orvieto) and by some transformations carried out in the 17C. 15C mullioned windows with two and four lights add grace and elegance to the **Bell Tower** which dominates the church. The **façade** has three portals, with a great central oculus and mullioned windows above the aisles.
The **interior,** divided into a nave and two aisles, is characterized by the cross vaulting above the nave. An outstanding feature is the **Paradisi Chapel** (14C), decorated with frescoes by Bartolomeo di Tommaso (15C) who was inspired by the *Episodes from the Divine Comedy.*

ENVIRONS

CASCATA DELLE MARMORE - *Historical Background* - The Cascata delle Marmore (Marble Waterfall), so-called on account of the incrustations of calcium salts, which resemble marble, is a remarkable feat of Roman hydraulic engineering. A channel was dug in order to drain the Rieti basin, diverting the River Velino into the Nera by means of a drop of 165 m. This first outlet was dug in 271 BC by M. Curio Dentato. In spite of the disputes which raged over its usefulness and fierce opposition on the part of those who believed it might constitute a threat for the city of Rome - which was subject to floods when the banks of the Tiber overflowed - the *Curiano Channel* remained in use until the beginning of the 15C, when the *Reati Canal* was built. This second channel was excavated because incrustations had formed along the first channel, thereby hindering the flow of water. Antonio da Sangallo the Younger was put in charge of the project to dig the *Paolino Canal*; at the turn of the 16C, it was decided to increase the depth of the old Curiano Channel and on this occasion Domenico Fontana built a regulating bridge which turned out to be of no useful purpose whatsoever. Under Pope Pius VI (at the end of the 18C) the so-called "diagonal cut of Pius VI" was completed, in order to limit the damage being caused in the Valnerina. Today the falls are visible only on certain days and at set times because they are used to produce hydroelectric power. They constitute an awe-inspiring show which merge splendidly with the surrounding natural scenery. Tourists and visitors can view the falls from two observation points: the **Lower Belvedere,** near a tunnel along the main Valnerina road, and the **Higher Belvedere,** which can be reached by turning off from the main road to Rieti. Anyone wishing to admire the waterfalls in full spate should contact the Tourist Promotion Board of Terni for a list of opening times and dates.

LAKE OF PIEDILUCO - The picturesque Lake of Piediluco, is the second largest lake in Umbria (Trasimeno being the largest) and it is situated in a beautiful natural setting, surrounded by wooded hills and mountains. The houses of Piediluco village situated along the shores of the lake and dominated by a 14C **Stronghold** are reflected in the transparent blue waters of the lake. The **Basilica of St Valentine** (Terni's patron saint) is just outside the town, on the site where the martyr is believed to be buried. It is thought that the 17C church was built on the site of a 4C Early-Christian place of worship.
In the 15C **Church of S. Maria del Monumento**, there is an interesting cycle of frescoes, inspired by the *Legend of the Golden Apples.*

Cascata delle Marmore near Terni, a spectacular view of the Lower Belvedere

Piediluco (Terni), two views of the picturesque lake surrounded by mountains

Todi, a panoramic view of the small town

TODI

HISTORICAL BACKGROUND - *An ancient, proud medieval city, it rises up in the midst of lovely hilly scenery on a hill dominating the confluence of the Naia into the Tiber. This particular setting emphasizes the rapport of continuity and integration that exists between the urbanized centre and the countryside. Probably founded by the Umbrian citizens of Veio, the ancient* Tutere *was certainly influenced by the Etruscans who had settled along the banks of the Tiber. It was Romanized around the mid-4C BC, and was known as* Tuder *in the Imperial age. Sacked by the Goths and Byzantines, it became a free Commune immediately after the year 1000. Having increased its power, it extended its dominion as far as Amelia (1208) and Terni (1217). From the second half of the 14C, it came under the rule of the Malatesta, Biordo Michelotti, the Anjous, Braccio Fortebraccio and the Sforzas. Successively, the city came under Papal control. The history of 16C Todi is dominated by the figure of Angelo Cesi, patron-bishop who did so much for the urban and monumental development of the city and for its revival after a dark period marked by plague and famine. An important administrative seat of the Department of Trasimeno under Bonaparte, it was assigned once more to the Pope of the post-Napoleonic restoration. An active participant in the fervent movement of the Risorgimento, it shared the fortunes of numerous other Umbrian centres, which ended up adhering to the new unitarian State.*
The city was the birthplace of Iacopo de Benedetti (1230-1306), better known as Iacopone da Todi, a Spiritual Franciscan, a great medieval poet who composed verses in Latin and in the Vernacular and the author of the renowned lauds. Most of this compact, habitable town is still contained within its ancient town walls, and the use of limestone brightens up many of the buildings in the centre. As well as the production of ceramics, majolica work and jewellery, the local handicraft industry is also renowned for the production and restoration of period furniture. Among the tasty tit-bits of the area mention should be made of pan nociato, bread made of sheep's cheese, walnuts and sultanas. Numerous festivities include; the Antiques Exhibition of Italy *(March-April)*, the National Trade Fair of Antiques *(June - July)*, the Festival di S. Maria della Consolazione *(8 September)*, the Todi Festival *(September)*, the feast day of the patron saint S. Fortunato *(14 October)* and St Martin's Fair *(11 November)*.

131

Todi, a view of the Renaissance Temple of S. Maria della Consolazione

TEMPLE OF SANTA MARIA DELLA CONSOLAZIONE - The first building to be seen by those approaching the town by motorway is the noble Renaissance church of Santa Maria della Consolazione. Its construction - undertaken on the site where there once stood a revered effigy of Mary subsequently called *S. Maria della Consolazione* - was begun in 1508 and was probably based on a design by Bramanti. The church was not completed until almost a century later and by that time most of the leading architects of the day, such as Peruzzi, A. da Sangallo and Vignola had had their say in its construction. The structure of the building, in the shape of a Greek cross, stands out because of its large central dome, built on an elevated tambour which is situated on a terrace with a balustrade. Underneath are the four apses, crowned by the same number of hemispheric calottes.
The large, splendid proportions of its light, airy **interior** do not detract from the essential simplicity of its architecture. One of its most outstanding features is the high altar which has four columns built of an-

Todi, the vault of the dome of the Temple of S. Maria della Consolazione

Todi, the beautiful façade of the Cathedral, flanked by a square-shaped bell tower

cient black marble. In all probability, it was designed by Andrea Polinori. At the high altar is situated the masterly 15C fresco of the *Maestà*(Majesty): the splendid Madonna della Consolazione which gives its name to the temple. The 17C sculptures of the *Apostles* were carved by artists from the workshop of Scalza.

CATHEDRAL - The construction dominates the monumental *Piazza Vittorio Emanuele* from the top of a flight of travertine steps. The most ancient parts of the church are the **Crypt** and the apse, both of which date back to the 8C. The present-day church, which was built near the Capitol on a spot which had been a sacred place of worship in Roman times, was originally built in the Romanesque style (12C). Subsequently, the addition of Gothic features (13C) radically transformed the appearance of the building. Work on the church was concluded in the 16C. The temple, dedicated to *S. Maria dell'Annunziata,* has a fine rectangular **façade**, partitioned by pilaster strips and mouldings and contains three rose windows (the sumptuous detail of the double rose window in the centre, is splendid) and the same number of Gothic portals. The present main façade, recently restored, replaces the original Romanesque one, and it is flanked by a robust 13C **Bell Tower** (previously used for defence purposes).

The basilica-like **interior** contains a nave and two aisles, even though another aisle was added in the second half of the 14C. On the counter-façade, there is a *Last Judgement* frescoed by Faenzone (Ferraù da Faenza, 16C). The left aisle contains some sculptures by Giovanni Pisano. In the smallest aisle are displayed paintings by Spagna and Giannicola di Paolo and a 15C font. In the apse, the walls of which contain 19C frescoes, there is a 13C *Cross* painted in the style of Giunta Pisano. Note also the precious wooden choir, executed by Antonio Bencivenni of Mercatello and his son (16C). The two paintings depicting *St Peter* and *St Paul* are the work of Spagna.

PIAZZA VITTORIO EMANUELE II - Called *Piazza Grande* in ancient times, it was probably located on the site of the Roman Forum and was much larger than the square which can be seen today. Counted as one of the most beautiful medieval squares in Italy, it is surrounded by numerous palaces and is dominated by the Cathedral.

Facing the latter, on the opposite side of the square, stands the turreted outline of the **Priors' Palace**. Several pre-existing buildings were amalgamated under one roof and the whole construction was completed in the first half of the 14C. At one time the seat of the *Priori* (Priors), it was subsequently the home of the Papal governors, which would explain the fact that it is also known as the *Palazzo del Governatore.* The mighty quadrilateral **Tower** was added in the second half of the 14C and was originally much higher than it appears today. The palace is crowned by Guelph crenellation. The windows of the two orders are the result of 16C transformations. The bronze *Aquila tuderte* (an eagle, symbol of Todi) which used to stand out over the second order was the work of Giovanni di Gigliaccio (1339).

The **Captain's Palace** is a 13C construction with a ground floor loggia and a broad flight of steps leading to the entrance. The **façade** is embellished with threefoiled, cuspidate, mullioned windows with three lights in the first order, while the windows of the second order which do not have cusps, are more in keeping with the Romanesque style. On the first floor there is a vast hall with two arches, decorated with coats of arms and fragments of frescoes. The building houses a museum.

The 13C **People's Palace**, is characterized by its Ghibelline crenellated crowning and is joined to the Captain's Palace by the same flight of steps. The **façade** is decorated by two orders of mullioned windows with several lights, whilst two large arches are situated on the ground floor.

ETRUSCAN - ROMAN MUSEUM AND TOWN PICTURE GALLERY - They are housed in the **Captain's Palace**. The Etruscan and Roman antiquities include numerous finds discovered at a necropolis in the district. Many terracotta objects (4C to 2C BC), votive bronzes and a collection of coins are just some of the exhibits which can be admired. There is also a copy of the *Todi Mars*, the original having been moved, along with other finds, to the Vatican Museums. Among the paintings in the Gallery, mention should be made of parts of a 15C triptych by Sienese artists, a *Crowned Virgin* by Spagna, and works of other Umbrian and Tuscan artists. Finally gold jewellery and antique ceramics are also displayed here.

CHURCH OF S. FORTUNATO - A splendid Gothic church built between the 13C and 15C on the site of a pre-existing place of worship dating back to the end of the 11C which had been annexed to a convent. The **façade** of the temple stands at the top of a spectacular, if somewhat steep, series of steps. The aim of accomplishing a marvellous decorative work is clear in the completed lower half; however, most of the upper order, which remains unfinished, has rough, coarse stonework. Of the three portals, the middle one is ogival in shape, markedly splayed and richly decorated. It is situated between the 15C sculptures of *Gabriel* and the *Virgin Mary*, attributed to a pupil of Jacopo della Quercia.

The majestic **interior,** which has a grandiose Gothic nave and two aisles of equal height, as well as fine cross vaulting, was recently restored and given several excessive coats of whitewash. In the right aisle there are some chapels with fragmentary frescoes painted in the style of Giotto. The fourth chapel has an outstanding 15C fresco (*Madonna and Angels*) by Masolino da Panicale. Behind the main altar, a 17C votive statue of *S. Fortunato* stands as a monument. In the apse, illuminated by large, mullioned windows with two lights is a remarkable late 16C choir finely carved by Antonio Maffei of Gubbio. The **Chapel of Our Lady of Loretto**, on the left, has 17C decorations and a wooden statue of the *Loretto Virgin*. The *Tomb of Iacopone da Todi* is in the **Crypt**.

FORTRESS - In the highest point of the city stand the scarse remains of this 14C fortification. After varying periods of prosperity and strife, the fortress was finally dismantled and demolished at the beginning of the 16C. On a clear day, marvellous views of the surrounding countryside can be enjoyed from the summit. Nearby the ruins of a Roman **Cistern** can be made out.

THE "NICCHIONI" (LARGE NICHES) OF THE ROMAN FORUM - Not far from the Etruscan **Marzia Gate** is the *Piazza del Mercato Vecchio* (lit. Old Market Square) upon which stand four huge niches similar to those supporting ancient medieval houses. It has been suggested that these niches constitute the remains of a temple consacrated to Mars, however this hypothesis does not seem likely. It seems more plausible that they were in actual fact the four apses of a Roman basilica. Note the Doric entabla-

Todi, the piazza Vittorio Emanuele II: in the background stands the embattled Priors' Palace, flanked by a quadrilateral tower. On the left, the People's Palace.

ture with its metopes and triglyphs. Interesting sections of a mosaic floor have unfortunately been covered with asphalt.

CHURCH OF SANT'ILARIO - Today the church is more widely known as the *Church of St Charles* - a name derived from the Fraternity of St Charles which was founded here in the first half of the 17C. The building was consecrated in 1249. The notable Romanesque stone **façade**, contains an unadorned portal and a simple, yet lovely rose window. On the crowning part of the building stands an airy, double-ordered bell-gable, with ornamental mouldings which are repeated along the main façade. The **interior** contains a fresco of the *Madonna del Soccorso*, by Spagna.

SCARNABECCO FOUNTAIN - The porticoed fountain, with basins and eight arcades, was constructed in the first half of the 13C at the behest of the Bolognese *Podestà* (the supreme medieval authority), Scarnabecco dei Fasiani.

CHURCH OF S. PRASSEDE - The church is an extremely ancient building which has an unfinished 15C **façade.** It is characterized by its two-toned stonework. A convent, which was once annexed to the church, belonged to the Augustinian order. In the first half of the 14C, the monks of this order transformed the church into a Gothic place of worship.

CHURCH OF S. NICOLÒ DE CRIPTIS - It is situated near the **Roman Gate,** which is set in the encirclement of the medieval **town walls**. This ancient building (end of 11C) was built over the ruins of the auditorium of the **Roman Amphitheatre** (the scarse remains of which can still be made out). Due to the numerous transformations which have taken place over the centuries, little now remains of the lay-out and features of the original construction.

***ENVIRONS* ·** The **Convent of Montesanto** dominates the town below and resembles a robust fortress. The building, which was constructed on a sacred Etruscan site, has, over the centuries, been both a place of worship and a strategic defensive outpost during the periods of strife between Todi and Orvieto. The church of the convent contains a noteworthy *Nativity* in the Umbrian style and frescoes by Cesare Sermei, an artist from Orvieto. The *Todi Mars* (currently in the Vatican) was discovered in this area.

TORGIANO

The most ancient town districts of Torgiano are situated on a small rise, dominating the point at which the Chiascio river flows into the Tiber, in the north-western part of the Valle Umbra. Due to its geographical position, on the fringe of the "Byzantine corridor" (which was the main communication and trading route between Rome and Ravenna) many battles were fought out here between various rival contenders. At the turn of the 13C, Perugia built a garrison here with the declared intent of guarding against any surprise attacks and also in order to defend the territories in its possession. Notwithstanding the strategic, military nature of this intervention, Perugia always respected the autonomous position of Torgiano. Just outside the town stands a **Tower (**bearing the municipal insignia) which once belonged to the Baglioni family and which today belongs to the town. The **Parish Church of St Bartholomew** has a lovely brick façade; although the origins of the church date back to the 13C, it was reconstructed in the 18C. The beautiful **Graziani-Baglioni Palace** dates back to the 17C. Its interior houses an interesting *Wine Museum* which provides visitors with an insight into the varied methods associated with viticulture and the wine-growing processes adopted in Umbria. The museum has some interesting pieces of equipment dating back to Etruscan and Roman times as well as the modern machinery used today. Furthermore, valuable Renaissance and 17C-18C majolica work can also be admired. The museum has a small collection of interesting books and documents on wine dating back to the 16C, including a section dedicated to the use of wine in pharmaceutical preparations.
Near Torgiano stands the ancient 8C. **Church of the Crucifix**, which was transformed during the Baroque period. Mention should also be made of the small village of **Pontenuovo** where a castle belonging to the Baglioni family once stood and the village of **Brufa** where the **Parish Church of S. Ermete** (formely the Priory of the Order of the Knights of the Holy Sepulchre) can be admired.

TREVI

A large medieval town which is situated on a green hill dominating the point at which the Clitunno river flows through the Valle Umbria. The first Umbrian settlements were established on the plain, on the site of the present-day Pietrarossa. After having become the Roman municipality of *Trebiae*, it expanded along both sides of the *Via Flaminia* and was a Lombard stronghold during the rule of the Dukes of Spoleto. Having become a free commune(13C), the town took an active part in the struggles between the powerful nearby cities of Perugia, Foligno and Spoleto. Around the mid 15C, it became part of the territory governed by the Church. Having obtained the status of a city from Pius VI (1784), it was annexed to the Kingdom of Italy in 1860.
Among the traditional festivals, mention should be made of the *Processione dell' Illuminata*,(27 January) on the eve of the patron saint's feast day of S.Emiliano, the *Tombola of the Town Districts* (a live tombola in costume, June) and the *Palio dei Terzieri*, a medieval contest with a historical pageant. (October).
The 14C **Town Hall** has a 15C portico and a 17C balcony. Numerous transformations were carried out between the 15C and 17C. At the side of the building stands the 13C stone **Torre Comunale** (Bell tower) crowned with corbels and four battlements. The bell itself dates back to the 16C.
The Town Hall houses the **Picture Gallery,** which includes archaeolgical finds dating back to the Roman period. Works by Spagna (*Coronation of the Virgin*), Pinturicchio (*Madonna and Child*), and Giovanni di Corraduccio (*Episodes from the Life of Christ*), are exhibited, along with a votive picture by pupils of Alunno, a painted 13C *Cross* and a *Crucifix* with 14C painting.
The Renaissance **Valenti Palace** stands out among the numerous palaces in the town which once belonging to the local aristocracy. Previously the home of an ancient, illustrious Trevi family, it has a façade decorated with a fine ornate portal. The charming internal courtyard has a portico, covered steps and well-head.

Trevi, a panoramic view of the town

The 13C **Church of St Francis** has Gothic features in the windows and side portals. The lunette over the main portal is decorated with a barely perceptible 14C fresco. The interior contains a 14C tomb of *Gioacchino Valenti* and the remains of another tomb of the same period. The walls are decorated with the remains of an ancient cycle of frescoes. Note also the 14C *Crucifix* in the apses (of the Umbrian school).

The ring of 13C **town walls** - actually the second urban encirclement - contains an extremely panoramic, circular **Tower**. The **Torrione della Neve** (Snow Tower), which is exposed to the north wind, takes its curious name from the time when it was used as an ice-house.

Built in the 12C, the **Church of S. Emiliano** has suffered as a result of the transformations carried out between the 15C to the 18C and again during the course of the 19C. Three apses from the original building are today visible on the right side. The fine 15C portal is crowned with a tympanum bearing precious high reliefs (*S. Emiliano among the lions*). In the interior, the beautiful Sacramental altar (16C), by Rocco di Tommaso from Vicenza, can be admired, together with a wooden statue portraying the *Patron Saint* (18C).

The so-called **Portico of Mostaccio** contains the remains of a gate which was set within the encirclement of the Roman walls. The round arch and the mullioned window above it were added in the 13C.

In the surrounding district stands the late 15C church of the **Madonna delle lacrime** (lit. of tears), which was given its name after a miraculous event occurred to the revered effigy of the *Virgin and Child* contained in its interior. The building was constructed to commemmorate the miracle which took place here. The church has a delightful Renaissance portal and contains paintings by Perugino (*Adoration of the Magi, St. Peter and St. Paul*), frescoes by Angelucci da Mevale and seven *Sepulchral Monuments to the Valenti* (16C to 17C).

The **Church of St Martin**, with its annexed convent, is situated in a beautiful panoramic position. The 14C building contains a fresco by Tiberio d'Assisi in the portal, while the interior has works by P. Mezzastris, one

Trevi, a view of the façade of the Small Temple of Clitunnus (also known as the Church of the Holy Saviour) and Theatre of Clitunnus

of the best-known exponents of the Folignio school of painters (*St Martin and the Beggar, Virgin and Child among the Saints and Angels*). Nearby is a chapel containing frescoes by Spagna and Tiberio d'Assisi.

On the site of the ancient Roman city, where the spas were probably situated; stands the **Church of S. Maria di Pietrarossa** (14C). The porticoed building has a wealth of frescoes and votive paintings dating back to the 14C and 15C (there are over 90).

In the small village of **Bovara** stands the note-worthy **Church of St Peter** (12C). The construction has kept some elements from the original Romanesque building - the rose window and bas-relief of the pediment. The interior, divided into a nave and two aisles, has the form of a basilica, but its linear features were distorted by the addition of a raised presbytery and an apse (14C). A wooden *Crucifix* (15C) is kept here.

The most important tourist attraction of the district around Trevi is the **Tempietto del Clitunno** (Small Temple of Clitunnus) (also known as the *Church of The Holy Saviour*), which lies in the Commune of Campello sul Clitunno. This is an Early-Christian temple (5C) which was constructed using material from the ruins of Roman buildings. Note the fine architectonic workmanship of this temple, with the pronaos and pediment supported by Corinthian columns. The murals contained in its interior (*Christ Omnipotent among the Angels* is worthy of note) are counted as being among the most ancient examples of Early-Christian art in Umbria (7C-8C).

FONTI DEL CLITUNNO - The Fonti del Clitunno (Springs of Clitunnus) are situated in a charming, picturesque setting. These springs were well-known as far back as ancient times: on this spot there once stood a temple dedicated to the oracular god Clitunnus. Other buildings were also consecrated to minor deities and the Roman *statio* of *Sacraria* was built along the Via Flaminia. An earthquake during the 5C upset many of the underground sources, thereby considerably limiting the flow of water. The tranquillity of the place and the beauty of the scenery which is characterized by numerous creeks and weeping willows mirrored in the little lake, have provided inspiration for many poets and scholars (among whom Virgil and Carducci). In the past, the water gushing from the living rock and numerous springs used to provide water-power for some nearby mills.

Springs of Clitunnus (Campello sul Clitunno), a picturesque view of the springs which have inspired many famous writers and poets

Umbertide, a view of the embattled towers which crown the mighty Fortress

UMBERTIDE

A town functioning as an important intersection point in the upper Tiber Valley, it boasts historical, cultural and artistic interest. The locality must have enjoyed a degree of importance even in ancient times, if it is true that it constituted a meeting and exchange point between the Etruscan and Umbrian populations along the banks of the Tiber. Little more than a village in the Roman age, when it was called *Pitulum,* it then disappeared under the devastation brought about by the Ostrogoths and by Totila. Risen up again as *Fratta* at the wish of the sons of Uberto, Marquis of Tuscany (end of 8C), it had an autonomous government until the second half of the 12C, when it was placed under the control of Perugia for defensive reasons. Almost a century later, it gave itself a free constitution and a stronghold was built in which Braccio Fortebraccio was imprisoned. Around the mid 16C, by Papal concession, the town was briefly entrusted to Paolo di Niccolò Vitelli. In 1643, Fratta opposed the Florentine besiegers, who were obliged to give up the venture, not without a heavy toll of casualties and considerable devastation. For a long time it remained under the control of the Church, with the exception of the brief Napoleonic interlude, and was integrated into the Kingdom of Italy in 1860. Three years later, it acquired the present-day name, to the everlasting memory of Uberto, father of the founders of the ancient Fratta. Today Umbertoide boasts an ancient tradition of the artisan craft of ceramics, as well as an excellent gastronomy. Among the various festivities, the August concerts of *Rockin' Umbria* and the celebrations on the occasion of the *Festa della Madonna* (8 September) are the most significant.

A turretted **Fortress** with battlements constitutes the most notable evidence of Mediaeval military architecture in the town. The building, girdled by mighty walls, has a large keep and three other towers, crowned with crenellations supported by corbels. Based on the designs of Trocascio (Angelo di Cecco), it was completed between 1374 and 1390.

The **Church of S. Maria della Reggia** (or *Regghia*) is a singular 16C domed construction on an octagonal plan. The circular interior is delightful, with Doric columns supporting the entablature on which the dome rests. A *S. Isidore* of the school of Reni (17C), an *Our Lady of the Assumption* by the 18C Perugian painter, G. Laudati, and a 15C fresco portraying the *Madonna and Saints* can be admired here.

Not to be forgotten are also the churches of **St Francis** (with annexed cloisters, 14C) and of **S. Croce** (17C) for the works of art they contain (*Madonna and Saints* by Pomarancio and the *Deposition* by Signorelli).

Finally, in the surrounding district, stands the notable **Montecorona Abbey**, founded by St Romuald (11C). In the church of the abbey, which has fine architectural features, and contains a nave and two aisles and a raised presbytery, there is an interesting 14C fresco (*Annunciation*). The beautiful crypt preserves Byzantine and Romanesque designs.

VALFABBRICA

The small villages which make up the Commune of Valfabbrica are scattered around a pleasant setting of green hills, in a territorial range which gravitates around the hydrographic basin of the Chiasco River. A dike above the town gave origin to the artificial dam of Valfabbrica. Previously mentioned as *Vado Fabrice* in the first half of the 9C, it was subjected to the Benedictine Monastery of S. Maria for a long time.

At Valfabbrica an artisan wood trade exists, while, among the more typical expressions of local folklore, mention should be made of the *Canto della Passione* (Lent) and the spring festival of the *Cantar maggio*.

The **Abbey-Church of St. Mary** was founded prior to the 11C. Previously the parish church of the village, it preserves some frescoes of the Umbrian school; another 15C fresco has been transferred to the modern **Parish Church**(1960). The turreted **Valfabbrica Castle,** restored after the 1971 earthquake, is all that remains of the ancient manor house.

In the small village of the same commune called **Casa Castalda, stands** an ancient **Castle**, believed to have been founded in the Lombard age (more specifically from the time of Desiderio's reign in the 8C). In the same village, the **Parish Church of S. Maria Assunta** contains a triptych with paintings of great worth, by Matteo da Gualdo and portraying an *Enthroned Virgin and Child among the Angels and Saints*. In the **Church of S. Maria dell'Olmo,** precious 15C and 16C frescoes, painted as offerings and attributed to Umbrian artists, are preserved.

VALTOPINA

The town, situated in the valley of the same name along which flows the Topino river, extends along the sides of the Via Flaminia, between Foligno and Nocera Umbra. Its remote origins date back to the second half of the 10C, when a colony of men from Apulia was founded here by the Duke of Spoleto, Pandolfo Testadiferro.

The craft industry of Valtopina produces ceramics and wrought ironwork. Some of the most characteristic festivities include the ancient festival of *Cantar maggio*, the *Festa della Madonna del Buon Consiglio* (the first Sunday in September) and the *Truffle Trade Fair* (November).

In the environs mention should be made of the ruins of the **Serra Castle**, founded in medieval times, and the **Poggio Castle**, of which only a mighty stone tower remains today. Ruins dating back to the Roman age have been discovered in the surrounding districts (**Forum, Rio Bridge**, and the **Parish Church of Fanonica**).

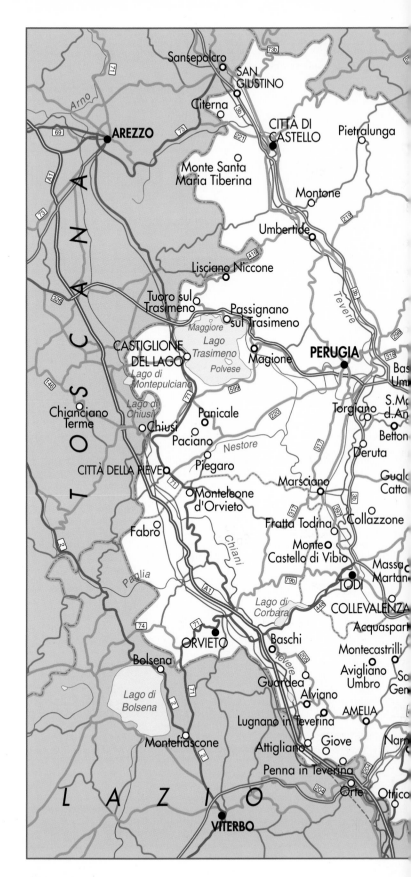

142

Autostrade
Strade statali di grande comunicazione
Altre strade statali
Strade d'importanza regionale
Ferrovie

MARCHE

SASSO-FERRATO
Scheggia e Pascelupo
M. Cucco 1566
Costacciaro
BIO
Sigillo
FABRIANO
MACERATA
Fossato di Vico
Gualdo Tadino
Potenza
alfabbrica
CAMERINO
ASSISI
1290 Monte Subasio
Nocera Umbra
Valtopina
SPELLO
nara
FOLIGNO
Bevagna
Visso
Montefalco
Sellano
Nera
Monti Sibillini
Trevi
Fti del Cliturno
Cerreto di Spoleto
Castelluccio
NORCIA
Tronto
Nera
Corno
Forca Canapine
SPOLETO
CASCIA
ROCCAPORENA
Monteleone di Spoleto
Ferentillo
Montefranco
Arrone
Polino
Leonessa
TERNI
PIEDILUCO
CASCATA DELLE MARMORE
Lago di Piediluco
ABRUZZO
Stroncone
Aterno
lvi dell'Umbria
RIETI
L'AQUILA

143

Index